The AS/400 Companion

The AS/400 Companion

by John Enck

and Michael Ryan

Printed in the United States of America.

Library of Congress Cataloging-in-Publication Data

Enck, John, 1956-
The AS/400 companion / John Enck and Michael Ryan.
p. cm.
Includes index.
ISBN 1-878956-45-0
1. IBM AS/400 (Computer) I. Ryan, Michael, 1957- . II. Title.
QA76.8.I25919E52 1994
005.4'3—dc20 94-24761
CIP

Please address comments and questions to the publisher:
CBM Books
1300 Virginia Drive, Suite 400
Fort Washington, PA 19034
(215)643-8000 FAX(215)643-8099

Editor: Carol Minton
Editorial Coordinator: Debbie Hiller
Production Manager: Patty Wall
Cover Design: Christine Minder

Contents

Acknowledgments

John Enck: To Marlene, Leanne, and Sean.

Michael Ryan: To Mom, Donna, and Tommy.

Introduction

COMPANION TO SUCCESS

When we wrote *Navigating the AS/400: A Hands-On Guide*, we sifted through the vast array of AS/400 features to find the key elements that made it tick. Given the sheer number of operating system (OS/400) commands, programs, and menus, this was a formidable task. We persevered and created a book containing approximately 450 pages of what we considered to be "must-know" AS/400 information. We are pleased with this book and consider it required reading for anyone interested in learning about the AS/400.

Sometime later we were asked to create a companion handbook to *Navigating the AS/400*. This handbook was to serve as a quick reference guide for those who have read *Navigating the AS/400* as well as for other AS/400 users. Once again we poured over all of the AS/400 commands, programs, and menus, but this time our goal was to present the minimum information that would provide maximum results when working with the AS/400.

Please note that this handbook is not a condensed version of *Navigating the AS/400*. In fact, we found some AS/400 topics that were inappropriate to cover in this focused handbook format: for example, user security, the System/36 environment, and other advanced topics that were too sensitive or intricate to cover lightly. For information on these topics, as well as a more in-depth look at the topics covered in this handbook, we strongly suggest you turn to *Navigating the AS/400*.

Does that mean you need *Navigating the AS/400* to fully appreciate this handbook? No. This handbook was designed to be a quick reference guide for all types of AS/400 users — application users, managers, programmers, and operators can all benefit from this easy-access information. Best of all, this handbook doesn't weigh down your briefcase so it can accompany you wherever you go. And since AS/400s are everywhere these days, you could be going places.

PRESENTATION CONVENTIONS

Keyboard keys are shown in uppercase letters between angle brackets: <ENTER>. Parameters requiring substitution are represented in lowercase letters between angle brackets: WRKOUTQ <queue name>. Optional parameters are shown between square brackets: DSPMSG [MSGQ(<queue name>)]. Commands that should be prompted using the <F4> key are noted with a leading exclamation mark: ! WRKSPLF.

CHAPTER 1

User Basics

SIGNING ON/OFF THE AS/400

The Sign On menu shows the current system, workstation, and subsystem assignments. Five data entry fields control the sign on process, as shown in Figure 1-1.

```
                          Sign On
                              System . . . . . :   S1027308
                              Subsystem . . . . :   QBASE
                              Display . . . . . :   PQMP00

           User . . . . . . . . . . . . . .  __________
           Password . . . . . . . . . . . .
           Program/procedure . . . . . . . . __________
           Menu . . . . . . . . . . . . . .  __________
           Current library . . . . . . . . . __________

                         (C) COPYRIGHT IBM CORP. 1980, 1991.
```

Figure 1-1: Sign On Menu

The User and Password fields allow you to enter your assigned user identification and optional password. The remaining three fields are optional and can be used as a shortcut to access a particular menu or program when your sign on is complete. After you input your user name, your password, and any of the optional fields, press the <ENTER> key. An X will appear in your workstation status line to indicate that you are inhibited from further input while the AS/400 verifies your user name and password.

If you want to run a specific program or procedure, specify the name of that program or procedure in the Program/Procedure field. To go to a specific menu, enter the menu name in the Menu field. (Note that if you specify an invalid menu name or program/procedure name, your sign on will be aborted and you will receive an error message.) To use a specific library as your default library when creating and locating objects, you can declare a library name in the Current library field. This field can be used in conjunction with the Program/Procedure field to run a program or procedure from a specific library.

Signing off can be accomplished two ways: by selecting Option 90 (Sign off) from either the AS/400 Main Menu or the OfficeVision/400 opening menu, or by entering the SIGNOFF command from a command line.

WORKSTATION USAGE

The 5250 family of AS/400 workstations covers a number of models, including the 5251, 5291, 3196, and 3197 workstations. All 5250 workstations are block mode devices, which means information entered on the screen is not sent to the application until you press <ENTER>, a function key, or some other trigger key. Minor operational differences exist between some of the 5250 models. This handbook shows the 319X series of workstations.

STATUS LINE

The bottom line of the 3197 status line display (Figure 1-2) contains the following indicators:

System Available — A block character indicates that the AS/400 is available.

Logical Display — This number indicates the logical display you are currently using. If your workstation supports two addresses, this number will change between 1 and 2 when you use the <JUMP> key.

Message Waiting (1) —This symbol indicates that messages are waiting on the message queue for logical display 1.

Message Waiting (2) — This symbol indicates that messages are waiting on the message queue for logical display 2.

Input Inhibited — An X indicates that the workstation will not accept any new input from you. This can occur when you are waiting for a response from an AS/400 command or program and you make a data entry or keyboard error. In the case of an error, the <RESET> key clears the error condition.

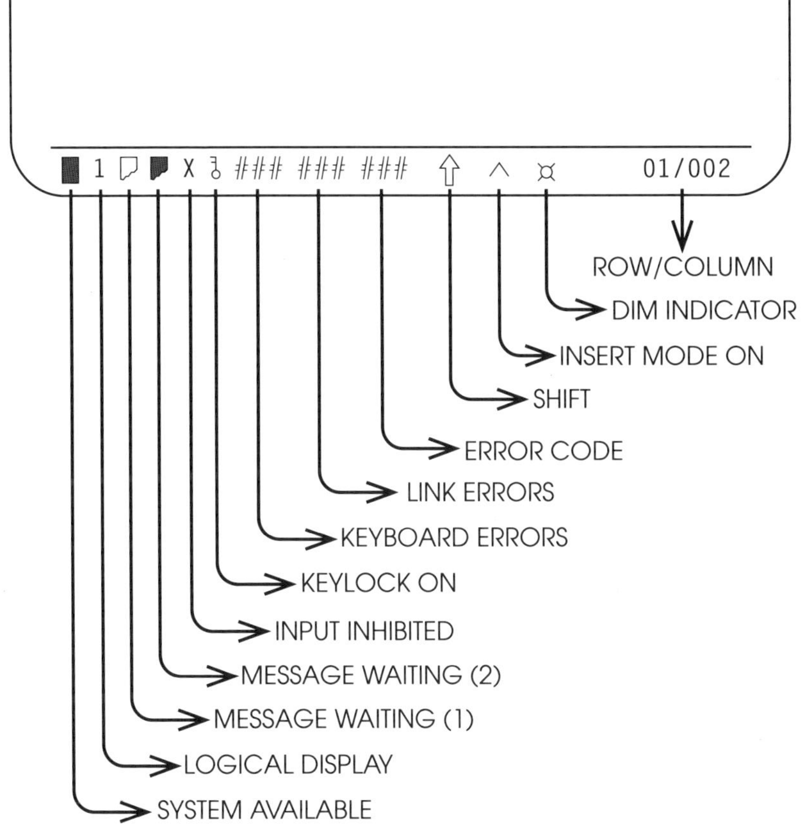

Figure 1-2: 3197 Status Line

Keylock On — This symbol indicates the physical lock on the workstation has been engaged and no keyboard input is allowed.

Keyboard Errors — If present, this number is a cumulative count of keyboard errors.

Link Errors — If present, this number is a cumulative count of communications errors.

Error Code — This position is one of several screen locations used to display error codes. Press <RESET> to clear the error.

Shift — This symbol appears whenever <SHIFT> key is pressed or after the <SHIFT LOCK> key has been pressed. Note that <SHIFT

LOCK> affects all of the alphanumeric keys, not just the alphabetic keys.

Insert Mode On — The circumflex symbol indicates that insert mode is on. When on, new characters are inserted at the current cursor location instead of overwriting existing information.

Dim Indicator — This symbol appears when the workstation automatically blanks the screen to protect it from phosphor burn. The screen can be restored by pressing any key. This feature can be disabled via setup.

Row/Column — The numbers in this position indicate the current row and column positions where the cursor is located. This feature can also be disabled via setup.

SYSTEM KEYS

The following 5250 keys perform system functions (Figure 1-3). The keys that work in conjunction with the <ALT> key are marked with an asterisk. Similarly, keys that work with the <SHIFT> key are marked with a circumflex.

<SYSRQ> — Invoke the System Request data entry line at the bottom of the screen. Enter a System Request function number or press <ENTER> for the System Request menu.

<ATTN> — Suspend the current operation and activate the default attention program.

<CLEAR> — Erase all input fields in the current screen and relocate the cursor to the first field.

<ERASE INPUT> — Erase the current input field and move the cursor to the beginning of that field.

<PRINT> — Send a copy of the current screen to the default output queue.

<HELP> — Bring up information about the current screen or current field.

<HEX>* — Generate a character based on the two-digit hexadecimal value entered after the <HEX> key is pressed.

<PLAY> — Play keystrokes assigned to function keys by the <RECRD> key function.

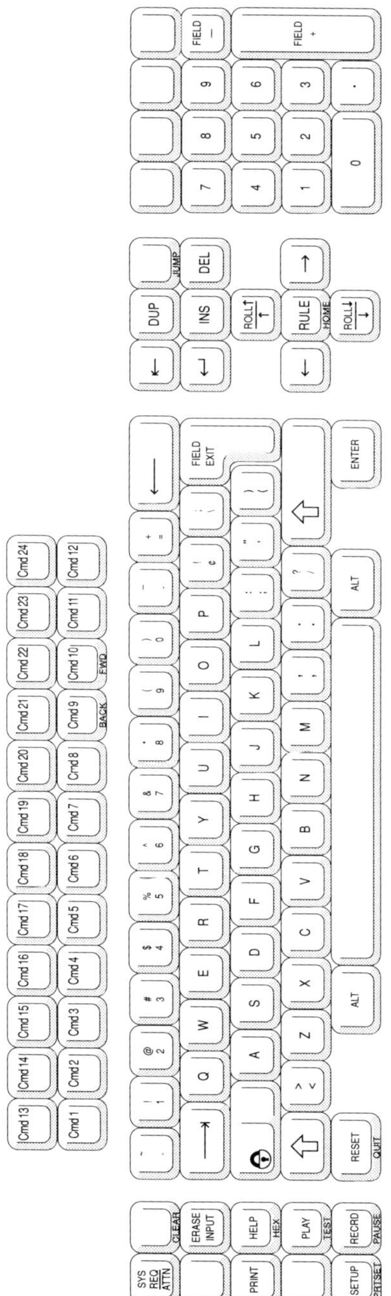

Figure 1-3: 3197 Workstation Keyboard

<TEST>* — Used for diagnostics.

<SETUP> — Define the operating characteristics for workstation.

<PRTSET>* — Define the attributes for an attached printer.

<RECRD> — Associate keystrokes with function keys.

<PAUSE>* — Use with the <RECRD> key to insert a pause into a keystroke sequence.

<FIELD ADVANCE> — Move the cursor from the current field to the next field.

<FIELD BACK> — Move the cursor to the beginning of the current field or to the beginning of the previous field.

<FIELD+> — Right-justify a positive number in a numeric field.

<FIELD-> — Right-justify a negative number in a numeric field.

<FIELD EXIT> — Use in alphanumeric fields to erase information in the current field that is behind and to the right of the cursor, and then advance the cursor to the next field. Also use in numeric fields to right-justify a numeric value and advance to the next field.

<SHIFT> — Use in conjunction with other alphanumeric keys to generate their shifted values.

<SHIFT LOCK> — Lock the alphanumeric keys into their shifted states. Press <SHIFT> to unlock.

<RESET> — Clear the workstation of error condition or terminate the Help, Insert, or System Request functions.

<QUIT> * — Use to terminate the Record and Play functions.

<ALT> — Use in conjunction with other keys to select functions shown on the front of key caps.

<ENTER> — Transmit the information contained in the data entry fields.

<BACKSPACE> — Perform a destructive backspace.

<DUP> — Request the application program to use the data from the last record entered in the current field.

<JUMP>* — Access the alternate logical display, if one is available.

<NEW LINE> — Move the cursor to the beginning of the first input field on the next line.

<INS> — Enter new characters at the cursor position.

<DEL> — Delete the character at the current cursor location.

<CURSOR UP> — Move the cursor up one row.

<CURSOR DOWN> — Move the cursor down one row.

<CURSOR LEFT> — Move the cursor left one character position.

<CURSOR RIGHT> — Move the cursor right one character position.

<ROLL UP> — Request the next screen in a multiscreen series.

<ROLL DOWN> — Request the previous screen in a multiscreen series.

<HOME>* — Move the cursor to the beginning of the first input field on the screen.

<RULE> — Turn on or off the ruler.

COMMAND/PROGRAM KEYS

The following function keys are commonly used while processing menus driven by standard AS/400 Command Language (CL) commands.

<F1> — Show help information for the command. The key can also be used for the same purpose.

<F3> — Exit the current command and return to the last major screen.

<F12> — Cancel the current command and return to the previous screen.

The following two function keys are commonly used when working with commands on the command line:

<F4> — Invoke parameter prompting for the command.

<F9> — Recall the previous command.

SETUP KEYS

The following function keys have the associated meanings while using the workstation setup function (accessed through the <SETUP> key):

<F2> — Select the ruler style.

<F3> — Set the automatic dim interval.

<F4> — Control the alarm volume.

<F5> — Set the clicker (key click) volume.

<F6> — Turn the clicker on or off.

<F7> — Toggle cursor blink on and off.

<F8> — Switch between block and underline cursor.

<F10> — Enable or disable extended code display.

<F11> — Turn the row/column indicators on or off.

<F12> — Toggle limited color mode on and off.

HELP FACILITIES

The OS/400 operating system provides assistance through the following functions and facilities: a context-sensitive <HELP> key; User Support and Education menu (GO SUPPORT); Search System Help Index (STRIDXSCH); and Online Education facility (STREDU).

THE <HELP> KEY

Basic information on most AS/400 menus and field items is available through the <HELP> key. The <HELP> key is context-sensitive. If you are viewing a standard menu and press the <HELP> key, you will see information about that menu. If, however, your cursor is located in a field on a data entry screen and you press <HELP>, you will see information about that specific field.

Help displays allow you to use the <ROLL UP> and <ROLL DOWN> keys to move forward and backward through the information. Function keys supported by help displays include:

<F2> — Display additional help, if available.

<F3> — Terminate the help display.

<F10> — Force the display to begin at a specific line by moving the cursor to a line on the display and pressing the <F10> key.

<F11> Search index — Invoke a search index function to scan for keywords.

<F12> — Terminate the help display.

<F13> — Go to the User Support and Education menu.

<F20> — Enlarge the help display area to consume more of the workstation screen.

<F24> — Show additional key functions.

USER SUPPORT AND EDUCATION

The User Support and Education menu contains a number of options to obtain additional information on AS/400 topics. Access the User Support and Education menu in one of three ways: enter 10 (User Support and Education) on the AS/400 Main Menu; press <F13> when a help display is on the workstation screen; or enter the command GO SUPPORT on a command line.

The User Support and Education menu features nine options, as shown in Figure 1-4. Note that all of these options may not be present on your display.

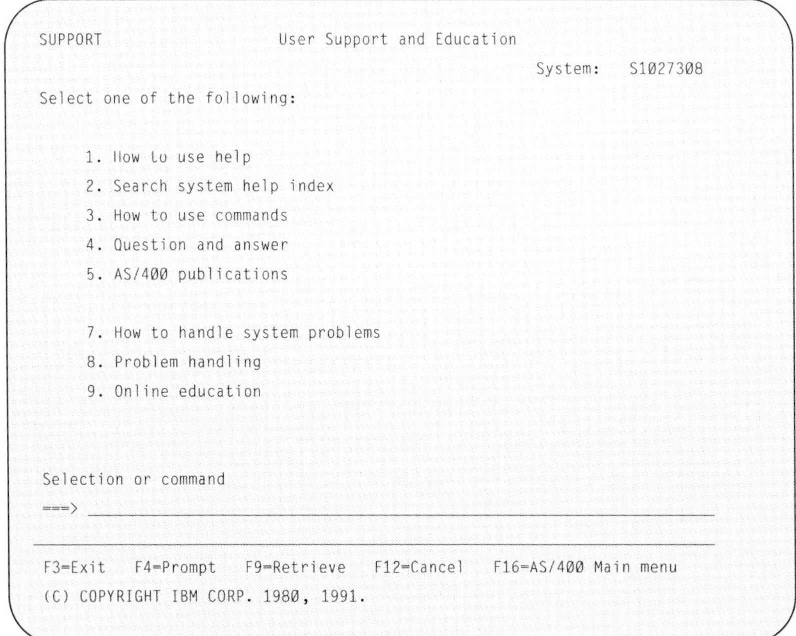

```
SUPPORT                  User Support and Education
                                                          System:   S1027308
Select one of the following:

     1. How to use help
     2. Search system help index
     3. How to use commands
     4. Question and answer
     5. AS/400 publications

     7. How to handle system problems
     8. Problem handling
     9. Online education

Selection or command
===> ____________________________________________________________

F3=Exit   F4=Prompt   F9=Retrieve   F12=Cancel   F16=AS/400 Main menu
(C) COPYRIGHT IBM CORP. 1980, 1991.
```

Figure 1-4: User Support and Education

Option 1 (How to use help) — Display narrative text on how to use the <HELP> key.

Option 2 (Search system help index) — Obtain help information based on keywords or phrases.

Option 3 (How to use commands) — Display narrative text on how to use AS/400 commands.

Option 4 (Question and answer) — Access a question-and-answer database that has been customized for your site.

Option 5 (AS/400 publications) — Show a list of the standard IBM documents.

Option 6 (IBM product information) — Initiate a communications link to a remote IBM system to look up information on new or existing IBM products and services.

Option 7 (How to handle system problems) — Display narrative text that explains the basic procedures used for handling problems.

Option 8 (Problem handling) — Invoke another menu that can be used to analyze and resolve operational problems.

Option 9 (Online education) — Start the online education module.

The options that display narrative text support the <ROLL UP> and <ROLL DOWN> keys to move through the text, and the <F3> or <F12> key to exit.

SEARCH SYSTEM HELP INDEX

The search help facility allows you to look for help information based on a keyword or phrase. Access the search help facility in three ways. Press <F11> from a display generated by the <HELP> key, select Option 2 (Search system help index) on the User Support and Education menu, or enter the STRIDXSCH command on a command line.

The Search Help Index menu provides a data entry area for you to enter your keyword or phrase. Alternatively, you may leave the data entry area blank and press <ENTER> for a complete list of index entries. Function keys that may be used with the Search Help Index include:

<F3> and <F12>— Leave the search index function.

<F5> — Display a list of all index entries.

<F13> — Go to the User Support and Education menu.

ONLINE EDUCATION

The online education facility provides intermediate and advanced training on a number of AS/400 topics. Access the online education facility in two ways: select Option 9 (Online education) from the User Support and Education menu or enter the STREDU command from a command line. Note that if you are using the online education for the first time, you will receive the Specify Your Name menu that asks for your first and last name. The Select Course menu then lists available courses. If more courses are available than can fit on your display, you can use the <ROLL UP> and <ROLL DOWN> keys to move through the list.

You can perform the following activities on a course from the Select Course menu:

Option 1 (Select) — Choose a course.

Option 5 (Display modules) — Display breakdown of course.

Option 8 (Display description) — Clarify contents and audience level.

The following keys are available within Online Education:

<ROLL UP> and <ROLL DOWN>— Move forward and backward through lists and text.

<F3> and <F12>— Terminate current menu operation.

<F17> and <F18> — Press <F18> to display the last (bottom) entries on the list of options. Press <F17> to return you to the top of the list.

<F9> — Send the list to your default print queue.

CHAPTER 2

System Interaction

OS/400 provides two types of interfaces that enable you to perform work: commands and menus.

OS/400 COMMANDS

Most OS/400 commands are composed of a verb component followed by a noun component. Some commands add a qualifier as a third component, and a few commands are simply a verb.

COMMAND VERBS

The top 10 verbs (in alphabetical order) are:

ADD — Add

CFG — Configure

CHG — Change

CPY — Copy

CRT — Create

DLT — Delete

DSP — Display

HLD — Hold

STR — Start

WRK — Work with

COMMAND NOUNS

The top 10 nouns (in alphabetical order) are:

F — Files

FLR — Folders

DOC — Documents

LIB — Libraries

OUTQ — Output queues

MSG — Messages

MSGQ — Message queues

SPLF — Spool files

SPLFA — Spool file attributes

WTR — Writers

COMMAND EXAMPLES

Some popular commands that exemplify the verb-noun construction include:

! **CPYF** — Copy file

! **DSPMSG** — Display messages

! **DSPSPLF** — Display spool file

! **HLDOUTQ** — Hold output queue

! **STRWTR** — Start writer

! **WRKF** — Work with files

! **WRKFLR** — Work with folders

! **WRKOUTQ** — Work with output queues

! **WRKDOC** — Work with documents

! **WRKWTR** — Work with writers

COMMAND ENTRY

Commands are normally entered on the command line located at the bottom of most screens. Commands the require no parameters can be started using the <ENTER> key. For commands that do require parameters, the values may be entered on the command line or command prompting can be invoked.

To enter parameters on the command line, specify the parameter name(s) followed by the corresponding value(s) enclosed in parentheses: COMMAND PARAM(VALUE) PARAM(VALUE). To prompt for command parameters, enter the command on the command line and press <F4>. A display containing available parameters appears. Press <ENTER> when all desired parameters have been entered or use any of the prompt function keys.

PROMPT FUNCTION KEYS

The following function keys are active when a prompted command display is present:

<F1> — Displays help for the command.

<F3> — Exits the command without execution.

<F5> — Refreshes the screen.

<F9> — Shows all possible parameters.

<F10> — Shows conditional parameters (based on parameters already entered).

<F11> — Displays keywords rather than a description parameters.

<F12> — Cancels the command and returns to the previous screen.

<F13> — Shows how to use command prompting.

<F14> — Displays the corresponding command line string based on parameters entered.

<F15> — Displays error messages.

<F16> — Suppresses additional parameter screens and executes the command immediately.

<F18> — Provides Double Byte Character Set (DBCS) conversion.

<F24> — Shows other keys available for this command.

Important note: If you are not sure if a command has parameters available, press <F4> instead of <ENTER>. Pressing <F4> can do no harm.

FINDING THE RIGHT COMMAND

OS/400 provides the SLTCMD (Select Command) command to help you search for commands (Figure 2-1). Entering SLTCMD without any parameters shows all available commands and entering SLTCMD with a partial name (SLTCMD WRK*, for example) produces a list of commands that begin with those characters.

```
                          Select Command

Type options, press Enter.
  1=Select

Opt  Command      Library     Text
 _   ADDAJE       QSYS        Add Autostart Job Entry
 _   ADDALRD      QSYS        Add Alert Description
 _   ADDAUTLE     QSYS        Add Authorization List Entry
 _   ADDBKP       QSYS        Add Breakpoint
 _   ADDCFGLE     QSYS        Add Configuration List Entries
 _   ADDCMNE      QSYS        Add Communications Entry
 _   ADDCNNLE     QSYS        Add Connection List Entry
 _   ADDDIRE      QSYS        Add Directory Entry
 _   ADDDLOAUT    QSYS        Add DLO Authority
 _   ADDDSTLE     QSYS        Add Distribution List Entry
 _   ADDDTADFN    QSYS        Add Data Definition
 _   ADDICFDEVE   QSYS        Add ICF Device Entry
                                                          More...
Parameters or command
===> ____________________________________________________________
F3=Exit   F4=Prompt   F5=Refresh   F9=Retrieve   F11=Display names only
F12=Cancel   F16=Repeat position to   F17=Position to   F24=More keys
```

Figure 2-1: Select Command

COMMAND RECALL

Command recall allows you to retrieve previously entered commands. Press <F9> to retrieve the previously entered command. The <F9> key can be repeatedly pressed to retrieve a command prior to the most current command.

OS/400 MENUS

Menus are an alternative way of running commands, as each menu option eventually executes a command. Menus display their name in the upper left corner of the screen. You may directly access these menus using the GO command.

There are two types of menus: OS/400 menus and user menus. OS/400 menus are part of the OS/400 operating system. User menus are created using the Screen Design Aid (SDA) utility. Virtually all OS/400 menus can be accessed by starting from the OS/400 Main Menu and working through subsequent menus and displays.

OS/400 MAIN MENU

The OS/400 Main Menu is displayed when you sign on to an AS/400, unless a custom menu has been substituted for the Main Menu (Figure 2-2). The authorization levels of the user determine which options will be shown. Therefore, all users may not have access to all options. The Main Menu can also be accessed using the GO MAIN command.

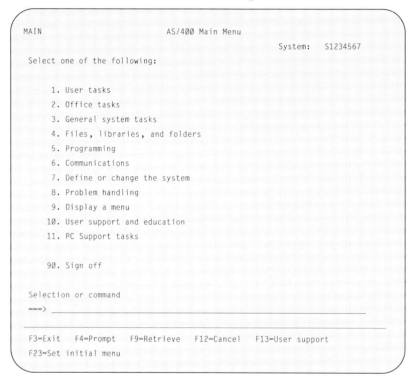

```
MAIN                          AS/400 Main Menu
                                                    System:   S1234567
 Select one of the following:

      1. User tasks
      2. Office tasks
      3. General system tasks
      4. Files, libraries, and folders
      5. Programming
      6. Communications
      7. Define or change the system
      8. Problem handling
      9. Display a menu
     10. User support and education
     11. PC Support tasks

     90. Sign off

 Selection or command
 ===> ____________________________________________________________

 F3=Exit   F4=Prompt   F9=Retrieve   F12=Cancel   F13=User support
 F23=Set initial menu
```

Figure 2-2: AS/400 Main Menu

The Main Menu can also be accessed using the GO MAIN command. The <F3> and <F12> keys will cancel the current menu and return to the previous menu. The total set of Main Menu options includes:

Option 1 (User tasks) — Shows the User menu (GO USER), which allows you to change your password and profile as well as work with your jobs, spool files, and messages.

Option 2 (Office tasks) — Displays the OFCTSK menu (GO OFCTSK), which allows you to access OfficeVision/400, utilize PC Support tasks, and perform other office-related functions.

Option 3 (General system tasks) — Shows the SYSTEM menu (GO SYSTEM), which enables you to work with different system functions, including jobs, devices, save/restore operations, messages, devices, and security.

Option 4 (Files, libraries, and folders) — Displays the Data menu (GO DATA), which allows access to file, library, and folder operations.

Option 5 (Programming) — Shows the Program menu, which permits access to programming activities such as programming debugging, utilities, and a special programmer's menu.

Option 6 (Communications) — Displays the CMN menu (GO CMN), which enables access to communications activities including network management, communications configuration, communications status, and sending/receiving files.

Option 7 (Define or change the system) — Shows the Define menu (GO DEFINE), which provides access to system configuration, security, operating system changes and fixes, and system values.

Option 8 (Problem handling) — Displays the Problem menu (GO PROBLEM), which provides access to system-level problem history logs, problem resolution utilities, and problem reporting tools.

Option 9 (Display a menu) — Executes the GO command to display a menu.

Option 10 (User support and education) — Shows the Support menu (GO SUPPORT), which allows access to OS/400 on-line education, the system help index, a publications reference, and user- level problem handling.

Option 11 (PC Support tasks) — Displays the PCSTSK menu (GO PCSTSK), which permits access to both user-oriented and administrative PC Support operations. User operations include working with documents and folders. Administrative options include user enrollment and PC Support configuration

Option 90 (Sign off) — Executes the SIGNOFF command.

TOP 10 COMMANDS

Any of the following commands (listed in alphabetical order) can be entered on the command line:

! **GO** — Access a specific menu.

! **CPYF** — Copy files.

! **DPSMSG** — Display messages.

! **SIGNOFF** — Leave OS/400.

! **SLTCMD** — Select command.

! **WRKACTJOB** — Work with active jobs.

! **WRKDIR** — Work with directory entries.

! **WRKDOC** — Work with documents in folders.

! **WRKOUTQ** — Work with an output queue.

! **WRKSPLF** — Work with spooled output files.

TOP 10 MENUS

Use the GO command to access any of these menus (shown in alphabetical order).

Assist — Operational Assistant

File — File tasks

Library — Library tasks

Main — OS/400 Main Menu

OFCTSK — Officevision/400 tasks

Subject — Commands in subject order

Support — User support and education

System — System maintenance tasks

User — User environment operations

Verb — Commands in verb order

CHAPTER 3

Libraries, Files, and Members

OS/400 uses libraries, files, and members as components to organize data. Libraries can also contain other objects (except for other libraries) used by the system and programs.

LIBRARIES

All AS/400 objects must reside in a library. There are three types of libraries on the AS/400: system libraries, which bear the attribute of *SYS and are considered part of OS/400; user libraries, which are owned or created by users or user programs; and product libraries, which are used in conjunction with commercial applications.

LIBRARY LIST

The library list is searched from top to bottom to find an object when a library name is not specified. The first occurrence of the object in the library list will be used. Note that many of the commands shown here will search the library list by default.

LIBRARY AND FILE WILDCARDS

You can specify special values to reference files and libraries. One special value is *ALL. This means that all files or libraries should be considered for the requested operation. Another special value is a generic file name, which ends with an asterisk. To specify a generic file or library name, enter the first few characters of the name and end the name with an asterisk. This will cause all files or libraries that have the same leading characters to come under consideration for the requested operation.

LIBRARY COMMANDS

To create a library —

CRTLIB LIB(<library name>)

Other common parameters —

TYPE(*TEST or *PROD)

TEXT('<descriptive text>')

To rename a library —

RNMOBJ OBJ(<library name>) +

OBJTYPE(*LIB) +

NEWOBJ(<new library name>)

To delete a library —

DLTLIB LIB(<library name>)

To clear a library —

CLRLIB LIB(<library name>)

To copy a library —

CPYLIB FROMLIB(<from library name>) +

TOLIB(<to library name>)

Other common parameters —

CRTLIB(*YES or *NO)

To display the contents of a library —

DSPLIB LIB(<library name> or *LIBL>) +

OUTPUT(* or *PRINT)

To work with libraries —

WRKLIB LIB(<library name> or *LIBL or <generic* name>) Figure 3-1 is an example of the Work with Libraries display:

```
                          Work with Libraries

 Type options, press Enter.
   2=Change    3=Copy    4=Delete     5=Display    6=Print
   8=Display library description      9=Save       10=Restore
   11=Save changed objects            12=Work with objects   14=Clear

 Opt  Library     Attribute    Text
 __   QSYS        PROD         System Library
 __   QSYS2       PROD         System Library for CPI's
 __   QUSRSYS     PROD         SYSTEM LIBRARY FOR USERS
 __   QHLPSYS     PROD
 __   QTEMP       TEST
 __   QGPL        PROD         GENERAL PURPOSE LIBRARY

                                                                    Bottom
 Parameters for options 2, 3, 5, 8, 9, 10, 11 and 12 or command
 ===> ________________________________________________________________________
 F3=Exit       F4=Prompt    F5=Refresh    F6=Create    F11=Display names only
  F12=Cancel      F16=Repeat position to      F17=Position to       F24=More keys
```

Figure 3-1: Work with Libraries

FILES AND MEMBERS

There are two types of files on an AS/400: database files and device files. A database file can be a physical file that contains data records or source statements or a logical file that contains access information for data. A device file describes the operational characteristics of a physical hardware device, such as a tape drive or printer.

Members are separate entities within a database file and are accessed through file commands. Database files can contain multiple members or a single member with the same name as the file.

DATABASE FILES

Physical files contain data or source statements stored in fixed length records. Physical files containing data records have an attribute of *DTA, while physical files that contain source statements have an attribute of *SRC. Logical files contain a view of the data contained in one or more physical files.

DATA DESCRIPTION SPECIFICATIONS

Creating database files usually requires that you define Data Description Specifications (DDS) for the file. The DDS for a file includes field names, lengths, access path information, select/omit criteria, and other attributes. DDS definitions are entered through the Source Entry Facility (SEU).

Database physical files can also be created by specifying a record length instead of using DDS. In this case, standard applications (such as SQL, PC Support, and others) will not be able to access fields in the file.

Creating the DDS does not create the file. A file is created with an appropriate Create command (CRTPF, for example). The Create command invokes the DDS processor, which checks the DDS source statements for correct syntax and produces a listing of the file layout and any errors encountered in the validation.

If the DDS contain no serious errors, the file will be created. Note that when the file is created, it will first delete any existing file of the same name. This will, of course, also delete any data in the file. Exercise caution before creating a new file so you do not unknowingly delete an existing file.

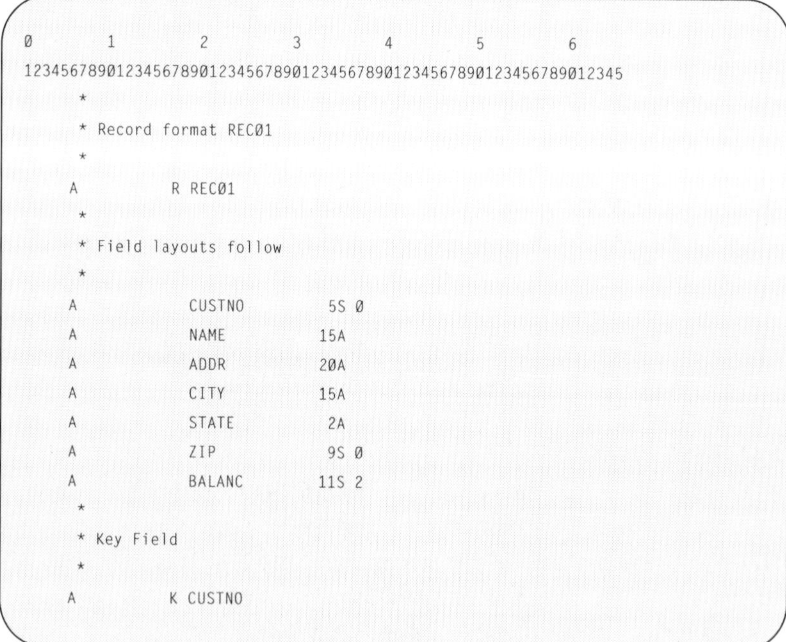

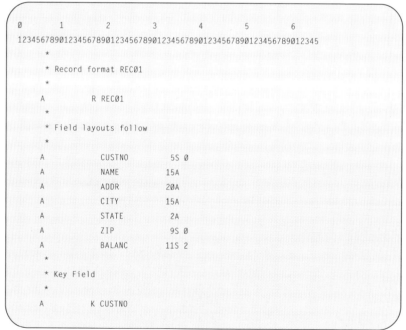

```
0        1         2         3         4         5         6
12345678901234567890123456789012345678901234567890123456789012345
      *
      * Record format REC01
      *
     A          R REC01
      *
      * Field layouts follow
      *
     A            CUSTNO         5S 0
     A            NAME          15A
     A            ADDR          20A
     A            CITY          15A
     A            STATE          2A
     A            ZIP            9S 0
     A            BALANC        11S 2
      *
      * Key Field
      *
     A          K CUSTNO
```

Figure 3-2: DDS Example

As shown in Figure 3-2, columns 1 through 44 of the source record contain the DDS positional entries and columns 45 through 80 contain the keyword entries. The source statements are in fixed format, and their use varies somewhat, depending on the type of file being created. All DDS records should contain the letter A in column 6.

The positional entries define the most common attributes of records and fields, such as names and length. One of the most common entries is the Specification Type in column 17. The Specification Type indicates whether the source record contains information about a record format, field name, key field, select or omit field, or join field.

Positions 19 through 28 contain the name of the field or record format. Positions 30 through 37 describe the type, length, and number of decimal positions for a field, while position 38 determines the field usage. The usage of a field determines if the field is input, output, both input and output, or a different usage for the field. In addition, if the file being described is a printer file or a display file, positions 39 through 44 define the location on the display or report.

Positions 45 through 80 of the source record contain the keyword entries. Keyword entries define the less common attributes, such as edit masks for output numeric fields, color and highlighting information for fields and literals in display files, and input editing for fields.

DEVICE FILES

Device files provide information regarding the characteristics of devices on the system. Device file types include printer files (*PRTF), which define the operational characteristics of printers; tape files (*TAPF), which define the operational parameters of magnetic tape drives; diskette files (*DKTF), which define the operational capabilities of removable (floppy) disk drives; and display files (*DSPF), which define the input and output handling between programs and user workstations.

COMMUNICATION FILES

Communication files facilitate the flow of information over a network. Communication file types include Inter-System Communication files (*ICFF), which enable programs residing on different host systems to communicate with one another, and Distributed Data Management files (*DDMF), which allow programs to open and access database files located on remote hosts.

FILE AND MEMBER COMMANDS

To create a physical file —

! CRTPF FILE(*CURLIB/<file name> or *LIBL/<file name> or <library name>/<file name>)

Other common parameters —

SRCFILE(*LIBL/QDDSSRC or <file name>)

SRCMBR(*FILE or <member name>)

RECLEN(<record length>)

TEXT('<descriptive text>')

To create a logical file —

! CRTLF FILE(*CURLIB/<file name> or *LIBL/<file name> or <library name>/<file name>)

Other common parameters —

SRCFILE(*LIBL/QDDSSRC or <file name>)

SRCMBR(*FILE or <member name>)

RECLEN(<record length>)

TEXT('<descriptive text>')

To create a source physical file —

CRTSRCPF FILE(*CURLIB/<file name> or *LIBL/<file name> or <library name>/<file name>)

Other common parameters —

TEXT('<descriptive text>')

To rename a file —

RNMOBJ OBJ(*LIBL/<old file name> or <library name>/<old file name>) +

OBJTYPE(*FILE) +

NEWOBJ(<new file name>)

To rename a file member —

RNMM FILE(*LIBL or <library name>/<file name>) +

MBR(<old member name>) +

NEWMBR(<new member name>)

To copy a file —

! CPYF FROMFILE(*LIBL/<from file name> or <library name>)/<from file name>) +

TOFILE(*LIBL or <library name>)/<to file name> or *PRINT)

Other common parameters —

FROMMBR(*FIRST or *ALL or <member name> or <generic* name>)

TOMBR(*FROMMBR or <member name>)

CRTFILE(*YES or *NO)

MBROPT(*REPLACE or *ADD)

To delete a file —

DLTF FILE((LIBL/<file name> or <library name>/<file name>)

To remove a member from a file —

RMVM FILE(*LIBL/<file name> or <library name>/<file name>) +

MBR(<member name> or <generic* name> or *ALL)

To clear a physical file member —

CLRPFM FILE(*LIBL or <library name>) +

MBR(*FIRST or <member name> or *LAST)

To display a file —

DSPPFM FILE(*LIBL/<file name> or <library name>/<file name>)

Other common parameters —

MBR(*FIRST or <member name>)

FROMRCD(*END or <record number>)

To list a file description —

DSPFD FILE(*LIBL/<file name> or <library name>/<file name> or *CURLIB/<file name> or <generic* name> or *ALL)

Other common parameters —

TYPE(*ALL or <information type>)

OUTPUT(* or *PRINT or *OUTFILE)

FILEATR(<file attributes>)

To work with files —

WRKF FILE(*LIBL/<file name or *ALL> or <library name>/<file name or *ALL>)

Other common parameters —

FILEATR(<file attribute>)

Figure 3-3 is an example of the Work with Files display:

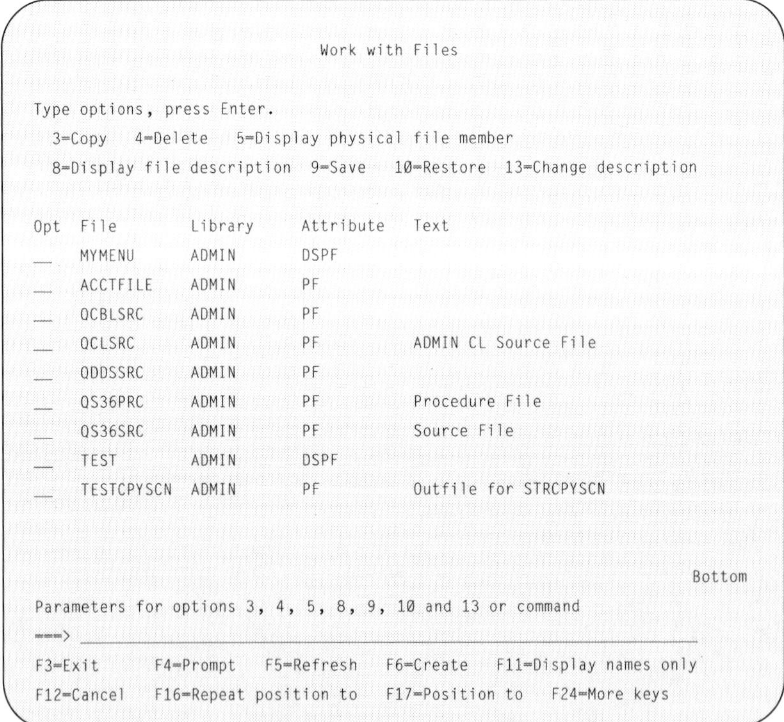

```
                              Work with Files

Type options, press Enter.
  3=Copy   4=Delete   5=Display physical file member
  8=Display file description   9=Save   10=Restore  13=Change description

Opt  File         Library     Attribute   Text
__   MYMENU       ADMIN       DSPF
__   ACCTFILE     ADMIN       PF
__   QCBLSRC      ADMIN       PF
__   QCLSRC       ADMIN       PF          ADMIN CL Source File
__   QDDSSRC      ADMIN       PF
__   QS36PRC      ADMIN       PF          Procedure File
__   QS36SRC      ADMIN       PF          Source File
__   TEST         ADMIN       DSPF
__   TESTCPYSCN   ADMIN       PF          Outfile for STRCPYSCN

                                                                   Bottom
Parameters for options 3, 4, 5, 8, 9, 10 and 13 or command
===> ____________________________________________________________________
F3=Exit       F4=Prompt   F5=Refresh     F6=Create     F11=Display names only
F12=Cancel    F16=Repeat position to     F17=Position to    F24=More keys
```

Figure 3-3: Work with Files

CHAPTER 4

Input/Output Queues

System messages and conversation messages from programs or other users are placed in message queues. Message queues are assigned to both users and workstations.

Printed output (reports, documents, and program listings, for instance) is directed to an output queue. When an output stream reaches the output queue, it becomes a spooled printer file. For a spooled printer file to leave the output queue and reach the printer, one final element is needed: a printer writer. A printer writer provides the interface between the output queue and the printer. All three elements — the output queue, the spooled printer file, and the printer writer — can be manipulated using OS/400 commands.

MESSAGE QUEUES

A message queue is simply a holding area for messages. You can display, delete, or reply to messages. Two types of message queues exist on an AS/400: user message queues and workstation message queues. Both types of message queues are assigned an OS/400 object type of *MSGQ.

A user message queue is a queue associated with a specific user. A user's message queue will be accessible to that user regardless of the terminal he or she is currently using. In contrast, a workstation message queue is associated with the terminal, not the user. A message sent to a workstation message queue is available to any user using that workstation.

MESSAGE QUEUE COMMANDS

To create a message queue —

! CRTMSGQ MSGQ([<library>/]<queue name>)

Other common parameters —

TEXT('<descriptive text>')

To delete a message queue —

DLTMSGQ MSGQ([<library>/]<queue name>)

To change a message queue —

! CHGMSGQ MSGQ([<library>/]<queue name>)

Other common parameters —

DLVRY(*HOLD or *BREAK)

To clear a message queue —

! CLRMSGQ MSGQ([<library>/]<queue name>)

Other common parameters —

CLEAR(*ALL or *KEEPUNANS)

To work with message queues —

WRKMSGQ MSGQ(<name or pattern> or *ALL)

To display messages —

DSPMSG [MSGQ(<queue name> or *SYSOPR)]

To send a message —

! SNDMSG MSG('<message text>')

Other common parameters —

TOUSR(<user name>, *ALLACT, or *SYSOPR)

To send a break message —

! SNDBRKMSG MSG('<message text>')+

TOMSQ(<message queue> or *ALLWS)

OUTPUT QUEUES

Output queues receive printed output generated from batch programs or from interactive sessions. Output queues are assigned a type of *OUTQ, and can reside in any library (although they will quite often be in library QGPL).

OUTPUT QUEUE COMMANDS

To create an output queue —

! CRTOUTQ OUTQ([<library>/]<queue name>)

Other common parameters —

SEQ(*FIFO or *JOBNBR)

TEXT('<descriptive text>')

To change an output queue —

! CHGOUTQ OUTQ([<library>/]<queue name>)

Other common parameters —

SEQ(*FIFO or *JOBNBR)

To clear an output queue —

CLROUTQ OUTQ([<library>/]<queue name>)

To delete an output queue —

DLTOUTQ OUTQ([<library>/]<queue name>)

To hold an output queue —

HLDOUTQ OUTQ([<library>/]<queue name>)

To release an output queue —

RLSOUTQ OUTQ([<library>/]<queue name>)

To work with output queues —

WRKOUTQ OUTQ(<name or pattern> or *ALL)

OUTPUT QUEUE STATUSES

The following status values are associated with output queues. These values can be seen using the WRKOUTQ command. See Figure 4-1.

```
                    Work with All Output Queues

 Type options, press Enter.
   2=Change   3=Hold   5=Work with   6=Release   8=Description

 Opt    Queue        Library        Files    Writer       Status
  _     ADMIN        QGPL               0                 RLS
  _     QDKT         QGPL               0                 RLS
  _     QPFROUTQ     QGPL               0                 RLS
  _     QPRINT       QGPL               0                 RLS
  _     QPRINTS      QGPL               0                 RLS
  _     QPRINT2      QGPL               0                 RLS
  _     QTIOUTQ      QTILIB             0                 RLS
  _     PRT01        QUSRSYS           19    PRT01        RLS
  _     PRT02        QUSRSYS            0                 RLS
  _     PRT03        QUSRSYS            0                 RLS
  _     QEZDEBUG     QUSRSYS            0                 RLS
                                                               More...
 Command
 ===> ____________________________________________________________
 F3=Exit   F4=Prompt   F5=Refresh   F12=Cancel   F24=More keys
```

Figure 4-1: Work with All Output Queues

HLD — The queue is held by a HLDOUTQ command. Spooled files will not print while in this state.

HLD/WTR — The queue is held but still has a printer writer attached. Spooled files will not print while in this state.

RLS/WTR — The queue is released and has a printer writer attached. This is the normal status for a functioning output queue.

RLS — The queue is released but does not have a printer writer attached. Spooled files will not print while in this state.

SPOOLED FILES

Spooled files hold the output that reaches output queues. Spooled files are sent from the output queue to a printer via a printer writer. If a printer writer is not attached to an output queue, spooled files will remain in that queue until they are deleted, or until a printer writer is attached.

Spooled File Commands

To display a spooled file —

! DSPSPLF FILE(<name>)

Other common parameters —

SPLNBR(<number>, *ONLY, or *LAST)

To hold a spooled file —

! HLDSPLF FILE(<name> or *SELECT)

Other common parameters —

OPTION (*IMMED or *PAGEEND)

To release a spooled file —

! RLSSPLF FILE(<name> or *SELECT)

To delete a spooled file —

! DLTSPLF FILE(<name> or *SELECT)

To change attributes of a spooled file —

! CHGSPLFA FILE(<name> or *SELECT)

Other common parameters —

OUTQ(<output queue name>)

COPIES(<number of copies>)

FORMTYPE(<form type>)

To send a spooled file to another system —

! SNDNETSPLF FILE(<name>)

Other common parameters —

TOUSERID(<user and address>)

To work with spooled files —

! WRKSPLF

Other common parameters —

SELECT(<user, device, etc.>)

SPOOLED FILE STATUSES

The following status values are associated with spool files (Figure 4-2). These values can be seen using the WRKOUTQ command.

```
                         Work with Output Queue

Queue:   PRT01           Library:   QUSRSYS         Status:   RLS/WTR

Type options, press Enter.
  1=Send  2=Change  3=Hold  4=Delete  5=Display  6=Release  7=Messages
  8=Attributes      9=Work with printing status

Opt File        User        User Data  Sts   Pages  Copies Form Type  Pty
 _  SETUPONECL ADMIN                   HLD      5       1   *STD        5
 _  QPJOBLOG    QSYS        QBASE      HLD    397       1   *STD        5
 _  QPJOBLOG    QSYS        QBASE      HLD      1       1   *STD        5
 _  QPJOBLOG    QSYS        SCPF       HLD     60       1   *STD        5
 _  QPJOBLOG    QSYS        QLUS       HLD      3       1   *STD        5
 _  QPJOBLOG    QSYS        QSYSARB    HLD      7       1   *STD        5
 _  QPJOBLOG    QSYS        QSYSARB    HLD      7       1   *STD        5
 _  QPJOBLOG    QSYS        QLUS       HLD      1       1   *STD        5
 _  QPJOBLOG    QSYS        SCPF       HLD     88       1   *STD        5
 _  QPJOBLOG    QSYS        QSPL       HLD      1       1   *STD        5
                                                                  More...
Parameters for options 1, 2, 3 or command
===> ____________________________________________________________________
F3=Exit   F11=View 2   F12=Cancel   F22=Printers   F24=More keys
```

Figure 4-2: Work with Output Queue

RDY — The spooled file is ready and available to be output to a printer.

OPN — A process has the spooled file open and is currently writing to it.

CLO — No more information is being written to the spooled file and OS/400 is in the process of closing the file.

HLD — The spooled file is in a held state and is not available for output.

SAV — The file has been sent to the printer but has been saved instead of deleted. The spooled file will remain in the output queue until explicitly removed.

WTR — The spooled file is currently being sent to the printer by the printer writer.

PND — The spooled file is in a pending state waiting for the printer writer to deliver it to the printer.

PRT — The spooled file has been sent to the printer but the printer writer has not finished its clean up work.

MSGW — The printer writer is processing the spooled file but requires a response to a message (message waiting) before it can proceed. This is often a forms related message.

***CHG** — The spooled file was changed using an option on the WRKOUTQ display.

***HLD** — The spooled file was held using an option on the WRKOUTQ display.

***RLS** — The spooled file was released using an option on the WRKOUTQ display.

PRINTER WRITERS

A printer writer is a job that normally runs in the QSPL subsystem. Each printer writer monitors a specified output queue. When spooled file entries are placed in an output queue, the writer will direct the spooled file to the printer device.

PRINTER WRITER COMMANDS

To start a printer writer —

! STRPRTWTR + DEV(<print device> or *SYSVAL or *ALL)

Other common parameters —

OUTQ(<queue name> or *DEV)

MSGQ(<queue name>, *DEVD, or *REQUESTER)

FORMTYPE(<type>, *ALL, *FORM, or *STD)

To stop a printer writer —

! ENDWTR WTR(<writer name>)

Other common parameters —

OPTION(*CNTRLD, *IMMED, or *PAGEEND)

To hold a printer writer —

! HLDWTR WTR(<writer name>)

Other common parameters —

OPTION(*CNTRLD, *IMMED, or *PAGEEND)

To release a printer writer —

! RLSWTR WTR(<writer name>)

Other common parameters —

OPTION(<number>, *CURRENT, *BEGIN, or *BYPASS)

To change a printer writer —

! CHGWTR WTR(<writer name>)

Other common parameters —

OUTQ(<queue name> or *DEV)

MSGQ(<queue name>, *DEVD, or *REQUESTER)

FORMTYPE(<type>, *ALL, *FORM, or *STD)

To work with printer writers —

! WRKWTR WTR(<writer name> or *PRT or *ALL)

CHAPTER 5

Operations

Operational tasks on an AS/400 include saving and restoring data, initializing media for use, and configuring devices. In addition, the Operational Assistant utility provides a convenient method of accessing operation functions.

SAVES AND RESTORES

OS/400 uses a single-level architecture that distributes all objects (including the operating system) across multiple physical disk drives and memory. Given this architecture, a hardware failure in a disk device can cause the loss of both operating system and business data. To minimize the risk of loss, the entire system should be saved on a regular basis. Information can be saved to tape, diskette, or a save file.

Saving the system consists of saving the licensed internal code, communication configuration objects, OS/400 required libraries, and security objects. Objects in user libraries (all non-OS/400 required libraries) must be saved separately.

THE SAVE PROCESS

To save the system —

SAVSYS DEV(<device>)

Other common parameters —

VOL(<volume ID>)

EXPDATE(*PERM or <expiration date>)

ENDOPT(*REWIND or *LEAVE)

CLEAR(*NONE or *ALL or *AFTER)

To save user libraries —

SAVLIB LIB(<library name> or *NONSYS or *ALLUSR or *IBM) +
DEV(<device> or *SAVF)

Other common parameters —

VOL(*MOUNTED or <volume ID>)

SEQNBR(*END or <sequence number>)

LABEL(*LIB or <label>)

EXPDATE(*PERM or <expiration date>)

ENDOPT(*REWIND or *LEAVE or *UNLOAD)

To save document library objects —

SAVDLO DLO(*ALL or *MAIL or *SEARCH or <DLO object name>) +
FLR(*ANY or <folder name>) + DEV(<device>)

Other common parameters —

VOL(*MOUNTED or <volume ID>)

SEQNBR(*END or <sequence number>)

LABEL(*LIB or <label>)

ENDOPT(*REWIND or *LEAVE or *UNLOAD)

To save objects —

SAVOBJ OBJ(<object name> or <generic* object name> or <list of +
object names> or *ALL) + LIB(<library name> or <list of library +
names>) + DEV(<device> or *SAVF)

Other common parameters —

OBJTYPE(*ALL or <object type> or <list of object types>)

VOL(*MOUNTED or <volume ID>)

SEQNBR(*END or <sequence number>)

LABEL(*LIB or <label>)

ENDOPT(*REWIND or *LEAVE or *UNLOAD)

Additional save commands —

SAVCHGOBJ — Save changed objects

SAVOBJ — Saving database files

SAVLICPGM — Save licensed programs

SAVSECDTA — Save security data

SAVSAVFDTA — Save save file data

SAVSTG — Save storage

The Restore Process

To restore a library —

RSTLIB SAVLIB(<library name> or *NONSYS or ALLUSR or *IBM) +
DEV(<device> or SAVF)

Other common parameters —

VOL(*MOUNTED or <volume ID>)

SEQNBR(*END or <sequence number>)

LABEL(*LIB or <label>)

ENDOPT(*REWIND or *LEAVE or *UNLOAD)

To restore objects —

RSTOBJ OBJ(<object> or <list of objects> or *ALL) +
SAVLIB(<library name>) + DEV(<device> or *SAVF) +
OBJTYPE(<object type> or *ALL)

Other common parameters —

OPTION(*ALL or *OLD or *NEW or *FREE)

RSTLIB(<new library name>)

Additional restore commands —

RSTAUT — Restore authority

RSTCFGOBJ — Restore configuration object

RSTDLO — Restore document library object

RSTLICPGM — Restore licensed program

RSTUSRPRF — Restore user profile

Save and Restore Media

Different save and restore commands can use different media. Here is the media type that can be used when saving information.

SAVDLO — Tape, diskette, save file

SAVCHGOBJ — Tape, diskette, save file

SAVLIB — Tape, diskette, save file

SAVLICPGM — Tape only

SAVOBJ — Tape, diskette, save file

SAVSAVFDTA — Tape, diskette

SAVSECDTA — Tape, save file

SAVSYS — Tape only

TAPE AND DISKETTE OPERATION

Tapes and diskettes are used on an AS/400 to save, restore, and copy information. Tapes and diskettes must be initialized before use. Initialization also assigns a volume identifier (a name given to a single tape or diskette, or a series of tapes or diskettes used for the same operation), an owner ID (identifies an owner), and a label (the name of the file (or object) as it is stored on the tape or diskette).

Tape and diskette operations use device files, an interface between the device and the system. Device files identify the tape or diskette unit to be used, and other characteristics such as the volume identifier, the label name, the type of file, the block and record length, the exchange type (for diskettes), and the code (EBCDIC or ASCII) to be used.

The standard naming convention for tape and diskette devices is TAPxx for tape devices and DKTxx for diskette devices, where the xx is the number of the device. The naming convention is determined by the value of system value QDEVNAMING.

To initialize a diskette —

! INZDKT DEV(<device>)

Other common parameters —

NEWVOL(<new volume ID>)

NEWOWNID(<new owner ID>)

FMT(*DATA or 1 or 2 or 2D or *DATA2 or *SAVRST)

SCTSIZ(*STD or 128 or 256 or 512 or 1024)

CHECK(*YES or *NO)

CODE(*EBCDIC or *ASCII)

To copy to a diskette —

CPYTODKT FROMFILE(*LIBL or <library name>/<from file name>) + TOFILE(*LIBL or <library name>/<to file name>)

Other common parameters —

FROMMBR(*FIRST or <member name>)

TOLABEL(*FROMMBR or <label name>)

TODEV(*DKTF or <device>)

TOVOL(*DKTF or <volume name>)

TOEXCHTYPE(*DKTF or *STD or *BASIC or *H or *I)

TOEXPDATE(*DKTF or *PERM or <date>)

NBRRCDS(*END or <number of records>)

To copy from a diskette —

CPYFRMDKT FROMFILE(*LIBL or <library name>/<from file name>) + TOFILE(*LIBL or <library name>/<to file name> or *PRINT)

Other common parameters —

TOMBR(*FROMLABEL or <member name>)

MBROPT(*NONE or ADD or *REPLACE)

Additional Diskette Commands

CHKDKT — Check diskette

CLRDKT — Clear diskette

CRTDKTF — Create diskette file

DSPDKT — Display diskette

OVRDKTF — Override diskette file

RNMDKT — Rename diskette

To initialize a tape —

! INZTAP DEV(<device>)

Other common parameters —

NEWVOL(*NONE or <new volume ID>)

NEWOWNID(*BLANK or <new owner ID>)

VOL(*MOUNTED or <volume ID>)

CHECK(*YES or *NO or *FIRST)

DENSITY(*DEVTYPE or <bits per inch>)

CODE(*EBCDIC or *ASCII)

ENDOPT(*REWIND or *UNLOAD)

CLEAR(*NO or *YES)

To copy to a tape —

CPYTOTAP FROMFILE(*LIBL or <library name>/<from file name>) +
TOFILE(*LIBL or <library name>/<to file name>)

Other common parameters —

FROMMBR(*FIRST or *ALL or <member name> or <generic* name>)

TOSEQNBR(*TAPF or <sequence number>)

TOLABEL(*FROMMBR or <label name>)

TODEV(*TAPF or <device>)

TOREELS(*TAPF or *SL or *NL or *LTM)

TORCDLEN(*FROMFILE or *TAPF or *CALC or <record length>)

TOENDOPT(*TAPF or *REWIND or *UNLOAD)

To copy from a tape —

CPYFRMTAP FROMFILE(*LIBL or <library name>/<from file name>) +
TOFILE(*LIBL or <library name>/<to file name> or *PRINT)

Other common parameters —

TOMBR(*FROMLABEL or *FIRST or <member name>)

FROMREELS(*TAPF or *SL or *NS or *BLP or *LTM)

FROMRCDLEN(*TAPF or *CALC or <record length>)

MBROPT(*NONE or *ADD or *REPLACE)

Additional tape commands —

CHKTAP — Check tape

CRTTAPF — Create tape file

DSPTAP — Display tape

OVRTAPF — Override tape file

VFYTAP — Verify tape

CONFIGURING LOCAL DEVICES

Local devices are configured automatically if system value QAUTOCFG is set to Y. A value of N requires that a device description be created for each newly added device. A number of different attachment types for workstation and printer devices are available. For example, you can attach twinax and ASCII workstations in addition to Token-Ring and Ethernet LAN attachments for PCs.

To configure a local workstation device —

CRTDEVDSP DEVD(<device description>) +
DEVCLS(*LCL or *VWS or *RMT)

Other common parameters —

TYPE(<device type>)

MODEL(<device model>)

PORT(<port number>)

SWTSET(<switch setting>)

ONLINE(*YES or *NO)

CTL(<controller description>)

KBDTYPE(*SYSVAL or <keyboard type>)

CHRID(*SYSVAL or <character ID>)

ALWBLN(*YES or *NO)

TEXT(<'descriptive text'>)

To configure a local printer —

CRTDEVPRT DEVD(<device description>) +
DEVCLS(*LCL or *VWS or *RMT)

Other common parameters —

TYPE(<device type>)

MODEL(<device model>)

AFP(*YES or *NO)

AFPATTACH(*WSC or *APPC)

PORT(<port number>)

SWTSET(<switch setting>)

ONLINE(*YES or *NO)

CTL(<controller description>)

PRTERRMSG(*INQ or *INFO)

MSGQ(QSYSOPR or <library name/queue name>)

TEXT(<'descriptive text'>)

OPERATIONAL ASSISTANT

Operational Assistant (OA) is an interface for system tasks such as managing user jobs and output, managing the system, performing backups, and performing system cleanup tasks. The actions performed via OA are the same as would be performed by executing operations system commands.

Different displays can be shown when using OA. Three command assistance levels are available that range from showing the command display or a less complex display. The assistance levels are:

***BASIC** — Provides basic, less complex displays.

***INTERMED** — For intermediate displays.

***ADVANCED** — Shows advanced displays.

OA is invoked via the GO ASSIST command to display the ASSIST menu. The Assist menu is shown in Figure 5-1.

```
ASSIST                  AS/400 Operational Assistant
                                                  System:   S1234567
To select one of the following, type its number below and press Enter:

     1. Work with printer output
     2. Work with jobs
     3. Work with messages
     4. Send messages
     5. Change your password


    10. Manage your system, users, and devices

    75. Documentation and problem handling

    80. Temporary sign-off


Type a menu option below
     ___

F1=Help   F3=Exit   F9=Command line   F12=Cancel
```

Figure 5-1: Assist Menu

Option 1 — Executes the Work with Spooled Files (WRKSPLF) command.

Option 2 — Runs the Work with User Jobs (WRKUSRJOB) command.

Option 3 — Invokes the Work with Messages (WRKMSG) command.

Option 4 — Sends a message to another user with the Send Message (SNDMSG) command.

Option 5 — Executes the Change Password (CHGPWD) command.

Option 10 — Displays the MANAGESYS menu to perform system maintenance-related activities. The MANAGESYS menu is shown later.

Option 75 — Documentation and problem handling, this option enables examination of online documentation, use of the system supplied help functions, and use of the online error determination and resolution facilities.

Option 80 — Temporary sign off, enables you to sign off the system temporarily.

The MANAGESYS menu is shown in Figure 5-2:

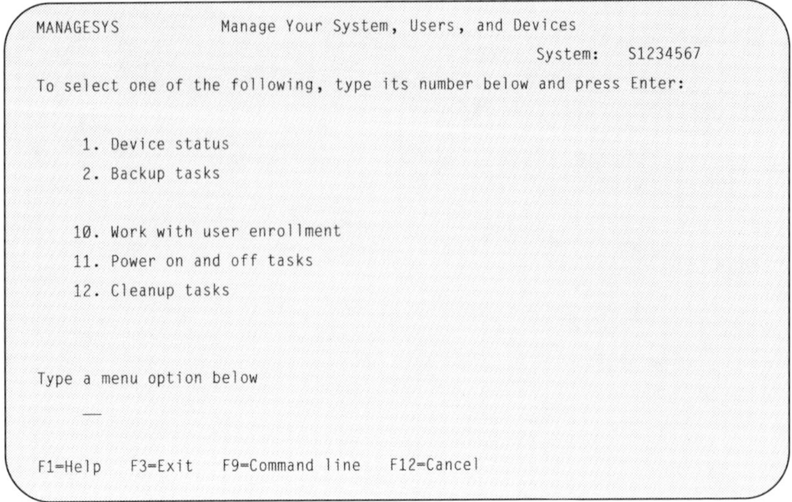

```
MANAGESYS          Manage Your System, Users, and Devices
                                              System:   S1234567
To select one of the following, type its number below and press Enter:

     1. Device status
     2. Backup tasks

    10. Work with user enrollment
    11. Power on and off tasks
    12. Cleanup tasks

Type a menu option below
   __

F1=Help   F3=Exit   F9=Command line   F12=Cancel
```

Figure 5-2: MANAGESYS Menu

Option 1 — Enables examination of device status with the DEVICESTS menu.

Option 2 — Provides backup of the system and user libraries. This option displays the Backup menu. This menu is shown later.

Option 10 — Works with user enrollment, which allows maintenance of directory and OfficeVision/400 enrollment entries.

Option 11 — Maintains a schedule of system power on and off events through the Power menu.

Option 12 — Displays the Cleanup menu to enable scheduling and execution of cleanup tasks.

The DEVICESTS menu is shown in Figure 5-3

```
DEVICESTS                     Device Status
                                                   System:   S1234567
To select one of the following, type its number below and press Enter:

     1. Work with display devices
     2. Work with printer devices
     3. Work with tape devices
     4. Work with diskette devices

    10. Print local device addresses


Type a menu option below
     __

F1=Help   F3=Exit   F9=Command line   F12=Cancel
```

Figure 5-3: DEVICESTS Menu

Option 1 — Work with display devices with the WRKCFGSTS CFGTYPE(*DEV) CFGD(*DSP) command.

Option 2 — Work with printer devices with the WRKCFGSTS CFGTYPE(*DEV) CFGD(*PRT) command.

Option 3 — Work with tape devices with the WRKCFGSTS CFGTYPE(*DEV) CFGD(*TAP) command.

Option 4 — Work with diskette devices with the WRKCFGSTS CFGTYPE(*DEV) CFGD(*DKT) command.

Option 10 — Print local device addresses with the Print Device Address (PRTDEVADDR) command.

The Backup menu is shown in Figure 5-4:

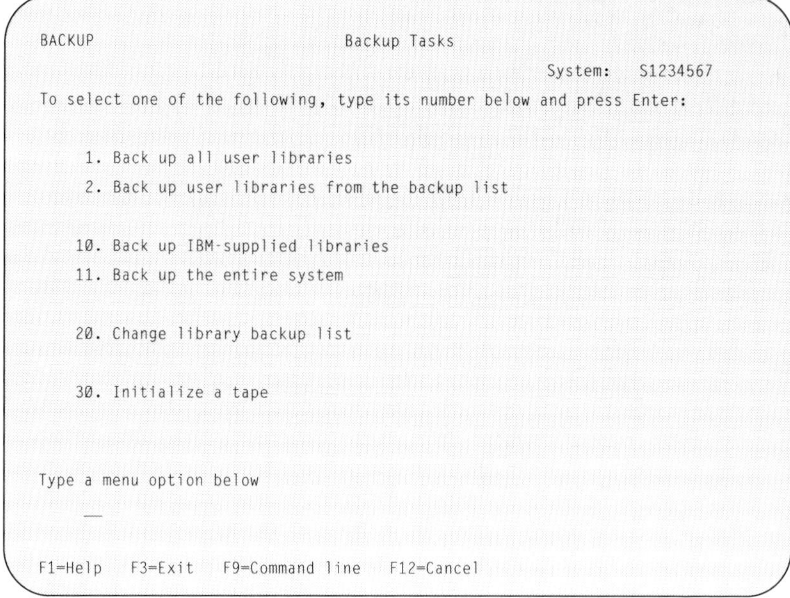
```
BACKUP                          Backup Tasks
                                                    System:    S1234567
To select one of the following, type its number below and press Enter:

     1. Back up all user libraries
     2. Back up user libraries from the backup list

    10. Back up IBM-supplied libraries
    11. Back up the entire system

    20. Change library backup list

    30. Initialize a tape

Type a menu option below
    _

F1=Help   F3=Exit   F9=Command line   F12=Cancel
```

Figure 5-4: Backup Menu

Option 1 — Back up all user libraries with the SAVLIB LIB(*NONSYS) command.

Option 2 — Back up user libraries from the backup list with the SAVLIB command, with the libraries contained in the backup list specified for the LIB parameter.

Option 10 — Back up the IBM-supplied libraries with the SAVLIB LIB(*IBM) command.

Option 11 — Back up the entire system with the SAVSYS command.

Option 20 — Provide a display upon which you can add or remove entries from the library backup list.

Option 30 — Initialize a tape with the Initialize Tape (INZTAP) command.

The Power menu is shown in Figure 5-5:

```
POWER                          Power On and Off Tasks
                                                        System:   S1234567
To select one of the following, type its number below and press Enter:

     1. Display power on and off schedule
     2. Change power on and off schedule
     3. Power off the system immediately
     4. Power off the system immediately and then power on


Type a menu option below
     _

F1=Help   F3=Exit   F9=Command line   F12=Cancel
```

Figure 5-5: Power Menu

Option 1 — Display power on and off schedule, which then displays Figure 5-6.

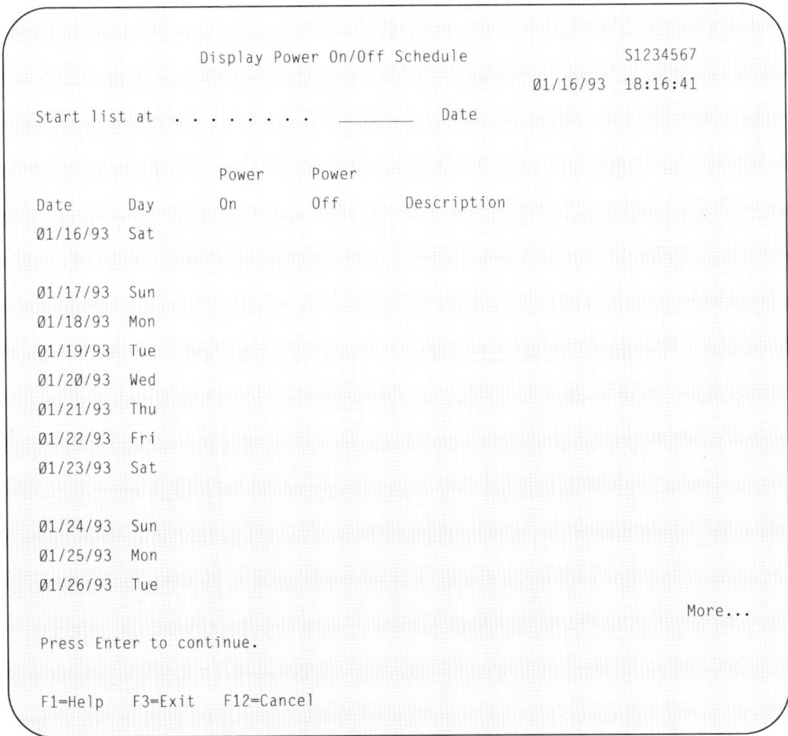

```
                    Display Power On/Off Schedule                 S1234567
                                                       01/16/93   18:16:41

Start list at . . . . . . . .  ________  Date

                          Power      Power
Date        Day           On         Off        Description
01/16/93    Sat

01/17/93    Sun
01/18/93    Mon
01/19/93    Tue
01/20/93    Wed
01/21/93    Thu
01/22/93    Fri
01/23/93    Sat

01/24/93    Sun
01/25/93    Mon
01/26/93    Tue
                                                                     More...
Press Enter to continue.

F1=Help   F3=Exit   F12=Cancel
```

Figure 5-6: Display Power On/Off Schedule

Option 2 — Uses the power schedule display to allow you to maintain the schedule.

Option 3 — Power off the system immediately with the Power Down System (PWRDWNSYS) OPTION(*IMMED) command.

Option 4 — Power off the system immediately and then power on with the Power Down System (PWRDWNSYS) OPTION(*IMMED) RESTART(*YES) command.

The Cleanup menu (Figure 5-7) is shown below:

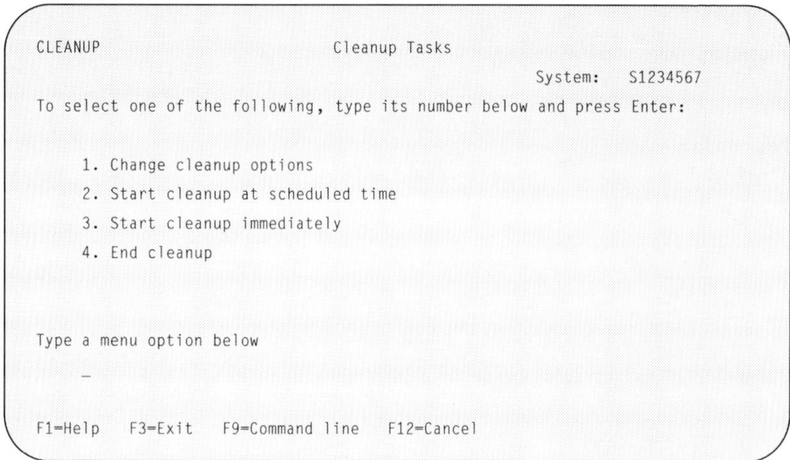

Figure 5-7: Cleanup Menu

Option 1 — Start or end scheduled cleanups, and change the time periods associated with different system items. This option displays Figure 5-8:

```
                         Change Cleanup Options                    S1234567
                                                          01/16/93  18:36:06
Type choices below, then press Enter.

Allow automatic cleanup . . . . . . . . . . . . .    Y        Y=Yes, N=No

Time cleanup starts each day  . . . . . . . . . 22:00:00      00:00:00-
                                                              23:59:59,
                                                              *SCDPWROFF,
                                                              *NONE

Number of days to keep:
  User messages . . . . . . . . . . . . . . . . .    7        1-366, *KEEP
  System and workstation messages . . . . . . . .    1        1-366, *KEEP
  Job logs and other system output  . . . . . . .    7        1-366, *KEEP
  System journals and system logs . . . . . . . .    30       1-366, *KEEP
  OfficeVision/400 calendar items . . . . . . . .    30       1-366, *KEEP


F1=Help   F3=Exit   F5=Refresh   F12=Cancel
```

Figure 5-8: Change Cleanup Options

The Allow automatic cleanup prompt determines if cleanup tasks will be executed. The Time cleanup starts each day prompt specifies when the cleanup tasks should execute. Special value "*SCDPWROFF" causes the cleanup tasks to be executed when the system is power cycled.

Option 2 — Schedules the cleanup process.

Option 3 — Causes the cleanup process to begin executing regardless of the scheduled time.

Option 4 — Removes the cleanup process from the schedule.

CHAPTER 6

Source Entry Utility

SOURCE ENTRY UTILITY OVERVIEW

The Source Entry Utility (SEU) is the primary text editor for the AS/400. SEU is used to edit members in source physical files.

INVOKING SEU

From the Main Menu, invoke SEU by selecting Option 4 (Files, libraries, and folders). After the Data menu appears, select Option 1 (Files). When the Files menu appears, select Option 4 (Edit a source file).

From the command line, SEU can be invoked through the Start Source Entry Utility (STRSEU) command, the Start Programmer Menu (STRPGMMNU) command, or through the Start Programming Development Manager (STRPDM) command.

The Start Source Entry Utility (STRSEU) command is used to directly access SEU. One of the important aspects of this command is that it remembers the last source file, library, and member you last edited. You are also able to select the source file and member by specifying the special value *SELECT for either of these prompts.

Other common parameters are SRCFILE(*LIBL or <library name>/<default based on type> or <file name>), SRCMBR(*SELECT or <member name>), TYPE(<member type>), and OPTION(<initial option>).

SEU TYPES

Specifying a type known to SEU allows syntax checking to be performed. The available SEU member types are:

BAS — BASIC language source; syntax checked.

BASP — BASIC procedure; syntax checked.

C — C language source; no syntax checking.

CBL — COBOL language source; no syntax checking.

CL — Command language source; syntax checked.

CLP — Command language procedure; syntax checked.

CMD — Command; syntax checked.

DFU — Data File Utility program; syntax checked.

DSPF — Display file DDS statements; syntax checked.

FTN — FORTRAN source; syntax checked.

ICFF — Intersystem Communication file DDS statements; syntax checked.

LF — Logical file DDS statements; syntax checked.

MNUDDS — DDS for menu; syntax checked.

MNUCMD — Commands for menu; no syntax checking.

MNU — Menu; no syntax checking.

PAS — Pascal source; no syntax checking.

PF — Physical file DDS statements; syntax checked.

PLI — PL/1 source; syntax checked.

PRTF — Printer file DDS statements; syntax checked.

QRY — Query/400 source; syntax checked.

REXX — REXX procedure source; no syntax checking.

RPG — RPG source; syntax checked.

RPT — Report source; syntax checked.

SPDCT — Spelling dictionary; no syntax checking.

SQLC — SQL statements for C source; no syntax checking.

SQLCBL — SQL statements for COBOL source; syntax checked.

SQLFTN — SQL statements for FORTRAN source; syntax checked.

SQLPLI — SQL statements for PL/1 source; syntax checked.

SQLRPG — SQL statements for RPG source; syntax checked.

TBL — SQL table definition; no syntax checking.

TXT — Text; no syntax checking.

An entry screen is presented when SEU is invoked to create a new member. Figure 6-1 shows the initial SEU screen for a new member. An existing member is displayed when selected.

```
 Columns . . . :    1  71            Edit                        ASOS/QRPGSRC
 SEU==> ____________________________________________________________    ASOSØ1
 FMT H  .....H........1..CDYI....S..............1.F............................
       *************** Beginning of data *************************************
''''''''
''''''''
''''''''
''''''''
''''''''
''''''''
''''''''
''''''''
''''''''
''''''''
''''''''
''''''''
''''''''
''''''''
''''''''
       ****************** End of data ****************************************

 F3=Exit   F4=Prompt   F5=Refresh   F9=Retrieve   F1Ø=Cursor
 F16=Repeat find       F17=Repeat change          F24=More keys
Member ASOSØ1 added to file ASOS/QRPGSRC.
```

Figure 6-1: SEU New Member

SEU is a full-screen editor, which means you can move the cursor around the screen to make changes. The <F4> key will prompt for a format in which to enter information. In addition, SEU prompting commands can be entered in the sequence number area. Note the command line at the top of the display. This can be used to enter the commands described later in this section.

FUNCTION KEYS

The following functions keys are available during SEU editing sessions:

<F1> — Help

<F3> — Exit

<F4> — Prompt

<F5> — Refresh

<F9> — Retrieve

<F10> — Cursor

<F11> — Previous record

<F13> — Change session defaults

<F14> — Find/Change options

<F15> — Browse/Copy options

<F16> — Repeat Find

<F17> — Repeat change

<F18> — DBCS conversion

<F19> — Left

<F20> — Right

<F21> — System command

<F23> — Select prompt

<F24> — More keys

EDITING OPERATIONS

For cursor and page movement, use the up and down cursor control keys to move to the previous or subsequent line. Use the left and right cursor control keys to move one character position to the left or right. Use the <ROLL UP> and <ROLL DOWN> keys to page through the member.

To insert a single line, enter I in the sequence number area. To insert multiple lines, enter In (where n is an integer) in the sequence number area. To input with prompt, enter IP in the sequence number area.

To input with format prompt, enter IPx (where x is a format code) in the sequence number area.

To copy and move lines, identify copy source and enter C (or CC at the beginning and end of a block) in the sequence number area. Identify mode source, enter M (or MM at the beginning and end of a block) in the sequence number area. Identify mode or copy target, enter a B (for before) or an A (for after) in the sequence number area.

To delete lines, enter a D (or DD at the beginning and end of a block) in the sequence number area. You can enter other line commands in the sequence number area. Here is a list of some line commands:

A, Ax — After

B, Bx — Before

C, Cx, CC, CR, CRx, CCR — Copy line

COLS — Display columns

D, Dx, DD — Delete lines

F, Fff, F? — Display format line

I, Ix, IF, IFx, IFff, IFffx, IF?, IF?x, IP, IPff, IP?, IS, ISx — Insert line

L, Lx, LL, LLx, LT, LLT, LLTx — Shift data left

M, Mx, MM — Move line

O, Ox, OO — Overlay

P, Pff, P? — Display prompt

R, Rx, RR, RRx, RT, RRT — Shift data right

RP, RPx, RPP, RPPx — Repeat line

S — Skeleton line

SF, SFx — Show first record

SL, SLx — Show last record

TABS — Set/display tabs

W, Wx — Window to line

X, Xx, XX — Exclude line

+, +x — Roll display forward

-, -x — Roll display backward

x — Go to line

FORMATS AND PROMPTS

Prompting provides a split-screen display where the upper part of the screen shows the statement being prompted and the lower portion of the screen is the prompt. Pressing <F4> (Prompt) or using the IP editing command allows statements to be prompted. The following screen (Figure 6-2) is shown when an IP or IP? command is entered:

```
                        Select Prompt

Type choice, press Enter.

  Prompt type . . . . . . . . . . . . . __      Values listed below

    RPG/400:          H,F,FC,FK,FX,U,E,L,I,IX,J (I cont),JX,DS,SS,SV,C,O,
                      OD,P (O cont),N,* (Comment)
    COBOL:            CB,C*
    REFORMAT/SORT:    RH,RR,RF,RC
    DDS:              LF (Logical file),PF (Physical file),
                      BC (Interactive Communications Feature file),
                      DP (Display and Printer file),
                      A* (Comment)
    MNU:              MS,MH,MD,MC (MD cont),CC (Comment)
    FORTRAN:          FT, F*
    Other:            NC (No syntax checking),** (Free format)

F12=Cancel   F23=Select user prompt
```

Figure 6-2: F23 Format Prompt

SEU COMMAND LINE OPTIONS

Commands can be entered at the SEU command line to find or change strings, save the member, or set environment options. Commands (and abbreviations, if available, that may be used are:

FIND (F) — Find a string.

CHANGE (C) — Change a string.

SAVE — Save the member.

CANCEL (CAN) — Cancel editing changes.

FILE — Save and exit.

TOP (T) — Go to member top.

BOTTOM (B) — Go to member bottom.

SET (S) — Set environment options.

- **MATCH** — Force a case match.
- **CAPS** — Only uppercase entry.
- **TABS** — Use tab settings.
- **ROLL** — Determines lines to roll.
- **EXPERT** — Use expert mode.
- **SHIFT** — Allows data to be shifted with a CHANGE operation.

FIND AND CHANGE FUNCTIONS

The Find and Change functions are accessed by pressing the <F14> key. The following Find/Change options screen (Figure 6-3) will be displayed:

```
                          Find/Change Options

  Type choices, press Enter.

    Find . . . . . . . . . . . . .   ________________________________
    Change . . . . . . . . . . . .   ________________________________
    From column number . . . . . .   1__          1-80
    To column number . . . . . . .   80_          1-80 or blank
    Occurrences to process . . . .   1            1=Next, 2=All
                                                  3=Previous
    Records to search . . . . . . .  1            1=All, 2=Excluded
                                                  3=Non-excluded
    Kind of match . . . . . . . . .  2            1=Same case
                                                  2=Ignore case
    Allow data shift . . . . . . .   N            Y=Yes, N=No

    Search for date . . . . . . . .  92/10/11     YY/MM/DD or YYMMDD
      Compare . . . . . . . . . . .  _            1=Less than
                                                  2=Equal to
                                                  3=Greater than

  F3=Exit   F5=Refresh         F12=Cancel   F13=Change session defaults
  F15=Browse/Copy options      F16=Find     F17=Change
```

Figure 6-3: Find/Change Options

Specify the value to search for in the first parameter, Find. This is the only required parameter. All others are optional. The Change parameter is used to change the found character string to a new string. The From column number and To column number parameters identify the beginning and ending columns in which to search.

The Occurrences to process determines the direction and number of occurrences for the search. The Records to search parameter determines which records to search. The Kind of match parameter determines the case checking of the search.

The Allow data shift parameter refers to changing information in the member if the information will be shifted as a result of the change. The Search for date parameter allows a search for the date information that is a part of every record of the member. The <F16> key (or <F17> key for changes) will search again with the same information.

UTILITY OPERATIONS

These options are accessible from the SEU editing screen by pressing <F15>. Figure 6-4 is the Browse/Copy Options display:

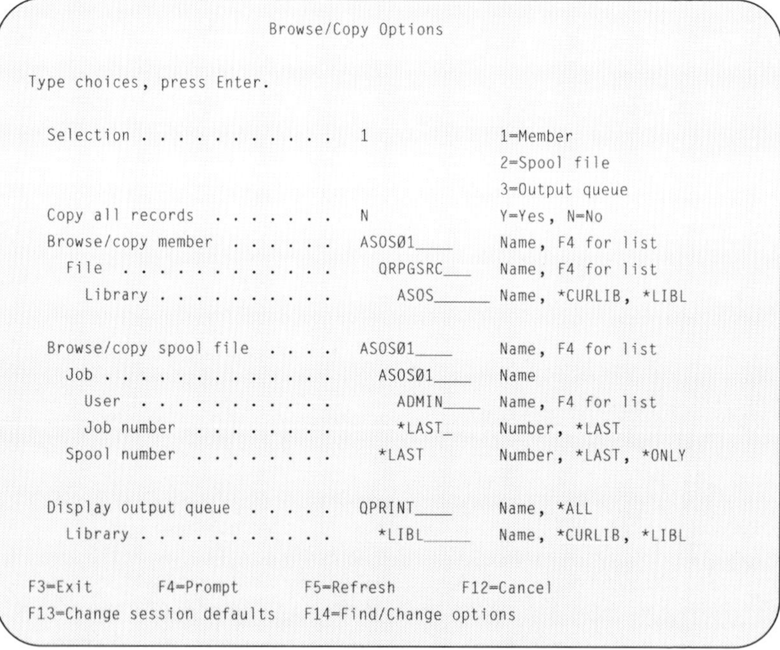

```
                         Browse/Copy Options

 Type choices, press Enter.

   Selection . . . . . . . . . . .   1           1=Member
                                                 2=Spool file
                                                 3=Output queue
   Copy all records  . . . . . . .   N           Y=Yes, N=No
   Browse/copy member  . . . . . .   ASOS01____  Name, F4 for list
     File  . . . . . . . . . . . .    QRPGSRC___ Name, F4 for list
       Library . . . . . . . . . .     ASOS______ Name, *CURLIB, *LIBL

   Browse/copy spool file  . . . .   ASOS01____  Name, F4 for list
     Job . . . . . . . . . . . . .    ASOS01____ Name
       User  . . . . . . . . . . .     ADMIN____ Name, F4 for list
       Job number  . . . . . . . .     *LAST_    Number, *LAST
     Spool number  . . . . . . . .    *LAST      Number, *LAST, *ONLY

   Display output queue  . . . . .   QPRINT____  Name, *ALL
     Library . . . . . . . . . . .    *LIBL_____ Name, *CURLIB, *LIBL

 F3=Exit        F4=Prompt          F5=Refresh         F12=Cancel
 F13=Change session defaults    F14=Find/Change options
```

Figure 6-4: Browse/Copy Options

The options are 1 to browse or copy another member, 2 to view a spooled file, or 3 to examine the entries in an output queue. Selecting 1 requires the Browse/copy member information to be completed. The Copy all records parameter refers only to copying a member. The default of N will allow you to specify a beginning and ending block of records to copy from the member. An entry of Y will copy all the records in the member. In either case, a target for the copy must be specified using the standard SEU target commands.

The Browse/copy member, with its associated file and library, identifies the member to be copied or browsed. The prompt key (<F4>) can be used to select a file if the library is specified, or a member if the file and library are specified.

Select the appropriate member and press <ENTER>. If the member is to be browsed or if all records are not to be copied, the screen will split horizontally. The original member is displayed on the top half of the screen and the member being browsed is displayed on the bottom half of the screen. The cursor can be positioned in the lower half of the screen and the <ROLL UP> and <ROLL DOWN> keys used to examine different portions of the member. The split display is shown in Figure 6-5:

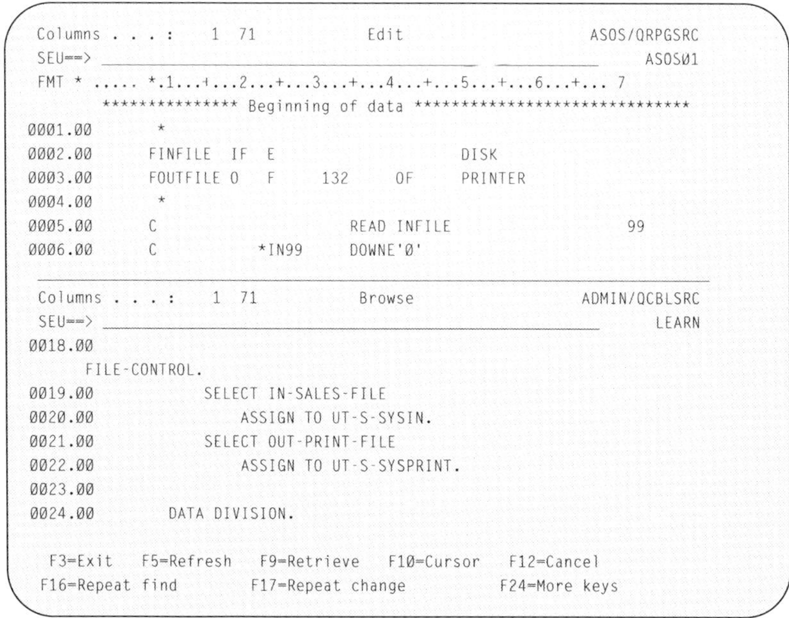
Columns . . . : 1 71 Edit ASOS/QRPGSRC
SEU==> ASOSØ1
FMT * ..... *.1...+...2...+...3...+...4...+...5...+...6...+... 7
*************** Beginning of data ******************************
ØØØ1.ØØ *
ØØØ2.ØØ FINFILE IF E DISK
ØØØ3.ØØ FOUTFILE O F 132 OF PRINTER
ØØØ4.ØØ *
ØØØ5.ØØ C READ INFILE 99
ØØØ6.ØØ C *IN99 DOWNE'Ø'
Columns . . . : 1 71 Browse ADMIN/QCBLSRC
SEU==> LEARN
ØØ18.ØØ
FILE-CONTROL.
ØØ19.ØØ SELECT IN-SALES-FILE
ØØ2Ø.ØØ ASSIGN TO UT-S-SYSIN.
ØØ21.ØØ SELECT OUT-PRINT-FILE
ØØ22.ØØ ASSIGN TO UT-S-SYSPRINT.
ØØ23.ØØ
ØØ24.ØØ DATA DIVISION.
F3=Exit F5=Refresh F9=Retrieve F1Ø=Cursor F12=Cancel
F16=Repeat find F17=Repeat change F24=More keys

Figure 6-5: Browse/Copy Split Screen

Records to be copied are specified by entering C or CC (for a block) in the line number area. The <F12> key will cancel the browse/copy operation.

Option 2 provides viewing of a spool file. An entry is required for the Browse/copy spool file parameter. The job name, user name, job number, and spool number can also be specified to identify the appropriate spool file. SEU defaults these parameters to values needed to identify a batch compilation of the member being edited.

The spooled file will be shown in the bottom half of the split screen and the member is displayed in the upper half of the screen in a similar manner to browsing a member. Navigation through the spooled file is also done in a similar manner.

Errors in a compile listing can be found when the spooled file is being displayed on the split screen. Search for errors by specifying *ERR as the search string on the SEU command line with the FIND command. This special option will search for error messages within a spooled file. The compiler error message is highlighted at the bottom of the screen, and second-level help can be obtained using the <HELP> key. This technique is great for finding errors and correcting the offending lines in a source member.

Option 3 of the Browse/Copy Options views the contents of an output queue. This selection executes the Work with Output Queue (WRKOUTQ) command. The Display queue (output queue) parameter is required. The corresponding optional library can also be specified.

CUSTOMIZING THE SEU ENVIRONMENT

Session environment values for the current SEU session can be changed by specifying commands on the SEU command line or by pressing <F13>. Figure 6-6 is an example of the Change Session Defaults screen accessed by using the <F13> key.

```
                        Change Session Defaults

 Type choices, press Enter.

   Amount to roll . . . . . . . . . . .   D__         H=Half, F=Full
                                                      C=Cursor, D=Data
                                                      1-999
   Uppercase input only . . . . . . . .   Y           Y=Yes, N=No
   Tabs on  . . . . . . . . . . . . . .   N           Y=Yes, N=No
   Increment of insert record . . . . .   0.01__      0.01-999.99
   Full screen mode . . . . . . . . . .   N           Y=Yes, N=No

   Source type  . . . . . . . . . . . .   RPG_______
   Syntax checking:
     When added/modified  . . . . . . .   Y           Y=Yes, N=No
     From sequence number . . . . . . .   _______     0000.00-9999.99
     To sequence number . . . . . . . .   _______     0000.00-9999.99

   Set records to date  . . . . . . . .   __/__/__    YY/MM/DD or YYMMDD

 F3=Exit      F5=Refresh   F12=Cancel
 F14=Find/Change options   F15=Browse/Copy options
```

Figure 6-6: Change Session Defaults

The Amount to roll option controls the number of lines that will scroll up or down when the <ROLL UP> or <ROLL DOWN> key is pressed. A value of H causes a half page roll, F causes a full page roll, C rolls leaving the cursor on the top or bottom line, and D rolls a full page minus 1 line. The SET ROLL line command can be used for this function.

The Uppercase only option determines the character case of entered information. A value of Y causes all characters entered to be in upper case, while a value of N allows both upper and lowercase entry. The SET CASE line command can be used for this function.

The Tabs on option determines if tab settings are used. A value of Y will enable tabs and a value of N (the default) will disable tabs. The SET TABS line command can be used for this function.

The Increment of insert option determines the sequence numbering for new lines added to the source member. You can specify a range of .01-999.99, with .01 being the default.

The Full screen option determines the available member viewing size. A value of Y instructs SEU to remove the function key legend and the format indication. The default is N, indicating the function keys and format will be shown. This function can be accessed via the SET EXPERT line command. The Screen size option identifies the screen size. A value of 1 indicates a 27 row by 132 column display, while a value of 2 refers to a 24 row by 80 column display.

The Source type option determines the source type SEU is using for syntax checking and prompting. Any valid SEU source type can be used. The Syntax checking option controls when and where syntax checking should be performed. A value of Y for the When added/ modified parameter causes syntax checking when the statements are added or modified. A value of N causes syntax checking to be performed when the member is saved. The From sequence number and To sequence number parameters establish the upper and lower bounds of line numbers to be syntax checked. Blank entries indicate all source statements should syntax checked.

The Set records to date option establishes the changed date for all statements in the member. The date must be specified in YY/MM/DD order. Press the <ENTER> key after you have changed the session environment options. These options will be in effect for the current SEU session.

Pressing <F21> causes a window to overlay the display. This window contains a system command line in which you can enter any valid OS/400 command. Use <F4> to prompt the command, the <F9> key to retrieve the previous command, and <F12> to cancel the window.

SAVING AND EXITING

Pressing the <F3> key produces the SEU exit display where you can save, create, or resequence the member and perform other utility operations. The save and cancel options that are available on this screen are also available with the SAVE and CANCEL line commands. Figure 6-7 shows the SEU exit screen:

```
                              Exit

 Type choices, press Enter.

   Change/create member . . . . . . . .  Y          Y=Yes, N=No
     Member . . . . . . . . . . . . . .  ASOS01____ Name, F4 for list
     File . . . . . . . . . . . . . . .  QRPGSRC___ Name, F4 for list
       Library . . . . . . . . . . . .     ASOS______ Name
     Text . . . . . . . . . . . . . . .  ________________________________
     Resequence member . . . . . . . .  N          Y=Yes, N=No
       Start . . . . . . . . . . . . .  0001.00    0000.01-9999.99
       Increment . . . . . . . . . . .  01.00      00.01-99.99

    Print member . . . . . . . . . . .  N          Y=Yes, N=No

    Return to editing . . . . . . . . .  N          Y=Yes, N=No

    Go to member list . . . . . . . . .  Y          Y=Yes, N=No

 F3=Exit   F4=Prompt   F5=Refresh   F12=Cancel
```

Figure 6-7: SEU Exit Screen

The Change/create member parameter defaults to Y if any changes have been made to the member. A value of N exits SEU without saving the member. The Member, File, and Library parameters specify the name and location of the member to be saved. The <F4> key can be used to prompt for the file or member name. The Text parameter is an optional 50 character text description associated with this member.

A value of Y for the Resequence member parameter causes SEU to resequence the line numbers. A value of N bypasses resequencing. The Start and Increment parameters specify the starting line number for resequencing and the sequencing increment.

The Print member provides for member printing. The default value of N causes SEU to not print the member when exiting. A value of Y will cause SEU to print the member and place the spooled file in your default output queue.

The Return to editing prompt normally defaults to N, indicating SEU will return to the command line or menu where SEU was invoked. An value of Y will be placed in this parameter if any syntax errors exist.

The Go to member list prompt defaults to N, which indicates that SEU will not display a member list. A Y value produces a list of members in the file. Change any information required and press <ENTER> to exit SEU.

PROGRAMMER MENU

The Programmer Menu provides access to several program development functions and is invoked with the Start Programmer Menu (STRPGMMNU) command. This menu is shown in Figure 6-8:

```
                          Programmer Menu
                                                   System:   S1234567
 Select one of the following:
       1. Start AS/400 Data File Utility
       2. Work with AS/400 Query
       3. Create an object from a source file       object name, type, pgm for CMD
       4. Call a program                            program name
       5. Run a command                             command
       6. Submit a job                              (job name), , ,(command)
       7. Go to a menu                              menu name
       8. Edit a source file member                 (srcmbr), (type)
       9. Design display format using SDA           (srcmbr), ,(mode)
      90. Sign off                                  (*nolist, *list)

 Selection . . . . .  _            Parm . . . .   __________
 Type  . . . . . . .  __________   Parm 2 . . .   _______________
 Command . . . . . .  ___________________________________________________
 ____________________________________________________________________________
 Source file . . . .  __________  Source library . . . . . . *LIBL_____
 Object library  . .  __________  Job description  . . . . . *USRPRF___

 F3=Exit        F4=Prompt        F6=Display messages    F10=Command entry
 F12=Cancel     F14=Work with submitted jobs            F18=Work with output
```

Figure 6-8: Programmer Menu

The Programmer Menu provides the following options:

Option 1 — Executes the Start Data File Utility (STRDFU) command to create, list, or update a data file.

Option 2 — Runs the Start Query (STRQRY) command to query a data file.

Option 3 — Creates an object from a source member. The appropriate create (CRT...) command is chosen by OS/400 based on the Type parameter.

Option 4 — Calls the program specified in the Parm field.

Option 5 — Executes the command specified in the Command prompt.

Option 6 — Submits the job specified in the Parm field. The submitted job will use the job description specified on the Job description parameter.

Option 7 — Displays the menu specified in the Parm field.

Option 8 — Invokes SEU. Optional parameters are the name of the member specified in the Parm field and the type of the member. Required parameters are the name of the Source file and the Source library.

Option 9 — Executes the Start Screen Design Aid (STRSDA) command to create, change, and test display files.

Option 90 — Executes the SIGNOFF command.

Special function keys on the Programmer Menu are <F6> to display messages (DSPMSG command), <F10> for the command entry screen (CALL QCMD command), <F14> to Work with Submitted Jobs (WRKSBMJOB command), and <F18> to Work with Output (WRKSPLF command).

CHAPTER 7

OfficeVision

OFFICEVISION/400 OVERVIEW

OfficeVision/400 is an office automation package that provides electronic mail, calendar, word processing, and other organizational aides for OS/400 users.

INVOKING OFFICEVISION/400

From the Main Menu, invoke OfficeVision/400 by selecting Option 2 (Office tasks). After the Office Tasks menu appears, select Option 1 (OfficeVision/400) to access OfficeVision/400. From the command line, enter the STROFC command to take you directly to the Main Menu, as seen in Figure 7-1. Note that you must be enrolled as a OfficeVision/400 user. Being able to sign on to the AS/400 does not automatically grant you access to OfficeVision/400.

```
                          OfficeVision/400
                                                    System:   DALLAS
Select one of the following:

     1. Calendars                                  Time:    5:18
     2. Mail
     3. Send message                            October          1992
     4. Send note                                S  M  T  W  T  F  S
     5. Documents and folders                                1  2  3
     6. Word processing                          4  5  6  7  8  9 10
     7. Directories/distribution lists          11 12 13 14 15 16 17
     8. Decision support                        18 19 20 21 22 23 24
     9. Administration                          25 26 27 28 29 30 31

    90. Sign off

                                               Bottom
Press ATTN to suspend a selected option.
Selection

    __

F3=Exit   F12=Cancel   F19=Display messages
(C) COPYRIGHT IBM CORP. 1985, 1991.
```

Figure 7-1: Main Menu

OFFICEVISION/400 FUNCTIONS

The standard implementation of OfficeVision/400 features nine primary options and a sign off option. Other custom options may be available. Because OS/400 allows for menus to be customized, all of the described options may not be available on your menu.

Option 1 (Calendars) — Maintain personal or group appointments.

Option 2 (Mail) — Work with mail you have received.

Option 3 (Send message) — Compose and send a brief (one or two line) message to another user.

Option 4 (Send note) — Use the OfficeVision/400 word processor to compose and send a short document.

Option 5 (Documents and folders) — Access documents stored in folders.

Option 6 (Word processing) — Access the OfficeVision/400 word processor.

Option 7 (Directories/distribution lists) — Manage lists of peoples names whom you may communicate with via electronic mail.

Option 8 (Decision support) — Access other, optional utilities.

Option 9 (Administration) — Change the environmental and authorization settings for your OfficeVision/400 interactions.

Option 90 Sign off — Exit OfficeVision/400 and sign off the AS/400.

SUSPENDING OFFICEVISION/400 FUNCTIONS

If you are using an OfficeVision/400 function and you need to return to the opening menu — for example, to read mail that has just arrived — you can suspend the current function using the <ATTN> key.

When you press the <ATTN> key, you will be returned to the opening OfficeVision/400 menu. Suspended functions will be marked by the > character appearing to the left of the option number, and the message ATTN pressed will appear above the selection field. You may then select another option, such as 2 to read new mail.

To return to a function you have suspended, select that option from the opening menu. You will be returned to your work-in-progress. Note: The <ATTN> key may be disabled in your user profile and therefore may not be available in OfficeVision/400.

LEAVING OFFICEVISION/400

You must use the opening menu to leave OfficeVision/400. If you are working within an OfficeVision/400 function, you can use <F3> or <F12> to exit that function and return to the opening menu. From the opening menu you can press <F3> or <F12> to leave OfficeVision/400, but remain signed on the AS/400 or select Option 90 to sign off the AS/400. This will automatically terminate your interaction with OfficeVision/400.

If you attempt to terminate your interaction with OfficeVision/400 and you have suspended functions that remain unresolved, an Exit OfficeVision/400 menu will appear asking if you want to abandon the suspended function(s). If you enter Y, all suspended functions will be terminated. If you enter N, you will be returned to the opening menu so you can properly terminate each suspended function.

CALENDAR

The calendar function allows you to view personal and group appointments from three perspectives: daily, weekly, and six month. Figure 7-2 is an example of a weekly calendar.

```
                             Weekly Calendar
Function . . . .  _________  Calendar . . . .  ENCK DALLAS____________
MON            TUE            WED            THU            FRI
10/12/92       10/13/92       10/14/92       10/15/92       10/16/92
8a__________   8a__________   8a__________   8a__________   8a__________
____________   ____________   ____________   ____________   ____________
9a__________   9a__________   9a__________   9a__________   9a__________
____________   ____________   ____________   ____________   ____________
10a_________   10a_________   10a_________   10a_________   10a_________
____________   ____________   ____________   ____________   ____________
11a_________   11a_________   11a_________   11a_________   11a_________
____________   ____________   ____________   ____________   ____________
12n_________   12n_________   12n_________   12n_________   12n_________
____________   ____________   ____________   ____________   ____________
1p__________   1p__________   1p__________   1p__________   1p__________
____________   ____________   ____________   ____________   ____________
2p__________   2p__________   2p__________   2p__________   2p__________
____________   ____________   ____________   ____________   ____________
3p__________   3p__________   3p__________   3p__________   3p__________
____________   ____________   ____________   ____________   ____________
4p__________   4p__________   4p__________   4p__________        More...
F3=Exit             F4=Prompt         F6=Add item          F9=Display item
F10=Change item     F12=Cancel        F16=Remove item      F24=More keys
```

Figure 7-2: Weekly Calendar

The following keys are active while in the calendar function:

<ROLL UP> and <ROLL DOWN> — Move the calendar forward and backward in time.

<F6> Add item, <F10> Change item, and <F16> Remove item — Alter the contents of the calendar.

<F9> View item and <F11> Change view keys — Alter how you look at calendar information.

<F13> More tasks — Additional calendar tasks.

<F15> Print — Allows you to specify print options and produce output.

<F19> Display message — Display your message queue.

<F21> Nondisplay — Reduces/expands the function key display on the bottom of the screen.

<F24> More keys — Pressing <F24> changes the function key display to show additional function keys.

CALENDAR SHORTCUTS

The main calendar display contains a field named Function, which may be used to enter a command to perform a specific function. A complete list of function commands can be obtained by pressing <F4> while the cursor is in the Function field. The most popular function commands are:

AE — Add event

AM — Add meeting

AR — Add reminder

VD — Change to daily perspective

VS — Change to six month perspective

VW — Change to weekly perspective

ELECTRONIC MAIL

OfficeVision/400 offers three options for handling electronic mail. Option 2 (Mail) allows you to read and review mail you have sent and received. Option 3 (Send message) allows you to send a two line electronic message. Option 4 (Send note) allows you to compose a brief document. Note that you are alerted to the presence of unread mail by the appearance of the message "New mail" on the OfficeVision/400 opening menu.

MAIL

When you select Option 2 (Mail) from the OfficeVision/400 menu, the Work with Mail display appears. New mail and any mail that you have received and not deleted will be listed on the display. On the left side of each mail item is a field where you can select an action to take on the item:

Option 2 (Revise a copy) — Copy the mail item into the OfficeVision/400 word processor so you can alter it and mail it out again.

Option 4 (Delete) — Remove the item from the list of mail items.

Option 5 (View) — See the contents of the mail item. You may use the <ROLL UP> and <ROLL DOWN> keys to page through the item as necessary.

Option 6 (Print) — Submit the mail item to a printer. Also see Option 9.

Option 8 (Change details) — Change some of the advanced aspects of the mail item.

Option 9 (Print options) — Submit the mail item to a printer after setting the variables that control how it will appear in print.

Option 10 (Forward) — Forward the mail item to an individual or group.

Option 11 (Reply) — Compose and send a note to the individual(s) who sent you the mail item.

Option 12 (File remote) — Save a note or document from the mail list to a folder located on another AS/400.

Option 13 (File local) — Save a note or document from the mail list to a folder on your AS/400.

Option 14 (Change authority) — Change the authority assigned to your filed documents.

Additional operations may be selected from the Work with Mail display through the use of function keys. The most popular operations are:

<F6> Outgoing mail status — Press <F6> to see the status of mail you have sent.

<F9> Action items — Pressing <F9> shows mail items that require action by a specific date.

<F13> More mail tasks — Pressing the <F13> key shows additional mail tasks.

SEND MESSAGE

Choosing Option 3 from the OfficeVision/400 opening menu brings up the Send a Message menu. This display (Figure 7-3) allows you to send a short message to one or more recipients. At the top of the form, you type the message you want to send.

```
                          Send Message

Type message.
________________________________________________________________
____________________________________________________________________
__________________________________________

Type distribution list and/or addressees, press F10 to send.
  Distribution list . . . . .  _______  _______  F4 for list

-----Addressees------
User ID     Address     Description
_______     _______
_______     _______
_______     _______
_______     _______
_______     _______
_______     _______
_______     _______
_______     _______
                                                            More...
F3=Exit     F4=Prompt   F5=Refresh   F9=Attach memo slip   F10=Send
F12=Cancel F13=Change defaults  F18=Sort by user ID F19=Display messages
```

Figure 7-3: Send Message

You can mail to a distribution list (a pre-defined list of users) and/or to one or more individual users. To send to a distribution list, enter its name in the first Distribution list field or press <F4> for a list of available distribution lists. The second field is optional and may be used to indicate the name of a different AS/400.

In addition to or instead of a distribution list, you may specify the user IDs (names) of individuals who are to receive the message. If you don't know what names are available, position the cursor in a name field and press the <F4> key. The optional Address field may be used to specify the name of another AS/400 where the user is located.

After you supply the user and any necessary address information, press the <ENTER> key. OfficeVision/400 will then verify the list of recipients. When all the information meets your satisfaction, press the <F10> key to send the message. Note: You must press the <F10> key to send your message.

SEND NOTE

If you want to send a communique that is longer than a message but not as lengthy as a formal document, select Option 4 from the OfficeVision/400 opening menu and the Send Note display appears.

At the top of the display you enter text for a Subject and a Reference in the designated fields. The rest of the fields are used to define the groups or individuals who will receive the message. When you are satisfied with the distribution information, press <F6> to call up the word processor's Edit display. This display (Figure 7-4) will contain the subject text, reference text, and distribution information you supplied.

Once you have entered your note, press the <F3> key to save the note and return to the Send a Note display. Then press <F10> to send the note to the designated recipients. Once again, you must press the <F10> key to send your message.

If your note is incomplete and cannot be sent, you may press <F17> (Save) and OfficeVision/400 will save your work in progress. You can complete the note at a later time by pressing <F16> (Work with saved notes) from the Send Note menu.

```
Insert Text        |                    |   |   |         |Pg 1
FMRX062416,*INTDOC                      |Typestyle 86 (12p)    |Ln 11
<.:..T.2..T.:..T.3..T.:..T.4..T.:..Tv5..T.:..T.6..T.:..T.7..T.:..T.8..T.>....9
F
TO:=         ==RYAN     DALLAS    Michael Ryan
=
FROM:=       ==ENCK     DALLAS    John Enck
=
DATE:=       =date=
SUBJECT:=  ==Sales Surge
REFERENCE:===Sales
R
=
== Start typing your note on the next line.=



=
=
 F1=Copy        F10=Send          F14=Get options       F21=Nondisplay keys
 F2=Move        F11=Insert lines  F16=Adjust/Paginate   F22=Spell functions
 F3=Exit/Save   F12=Cancel        F17=Functions         F23=Word spell aid
```

Figure 7-4:Send Note

DOCUMENT HANDLING

Option 5 (Documents and folders) and Option 6 (Word processing) on the OfficeVision/400 opening menu are the two functions provided for the creation and maintenance of documents. Both options allow you to access documents in folders. Option 5 gives you an administrative view of folders and documents while Option 6 (Word processing) allows you to create or edit a document stored in a folder.

DOCUMENTS AND FOLDERS

Option 5 on the OfficeVision/400 opening menu lets you peruse documents and folders you are authorized to access. From the Documents and Folders menu, you can select one of the following functions:

Option 1 (Work with documents in folders) — View and manage documents within a selected folder.

Option 2 (Work with folders) — View the folders available to you, access documents within those folders.

Option 3 (Search for documents) — Search for one or more documents based on qualifications such as subject, author, or keywords associated with the document. A list of qualifying documents is produced.

Option 4 (Work with document lists) — Access the lists created by Option 3.

WORD PROCESSING

If you select Option 6 from the opening menu, the Word Processing menu appears. Note that several of the options overlap the options available through the Documents and folders function (Option 5).

Option 1 (Work with documents in folders) — Create new documents or edit existing ones.

Option 2 (Work with documents to be printed) — See what documents are currently printing or scheduled to be printed.

Option 3 (Work with folders) — View the folders available and access documents within those folders.

Option 4 (Work with nontext document data) — Work with graphics created with the Business Graphics Utility (BGU) or some other graphics program.

Option 5 (Work with text profiles) — Establish or maintain profiles to control the layout and appearance of documents.

WORK WITH DOCUMENTS IN FOLDERS

When you select Option 1 from the Documents and Folders menu or the Word Processor menu, the Work with Documents in Folders menu appears, as shown in Figure 7-5.

At the top of the display is a field named Folder. This is the name of the folder containing the documents that appear on the display. To open a different folder, change the name in this field and press <ENTER>. If you enter the initial character(s) in a document name in the optional Position to field and press <ENTER>, the first matching document will appear as the first document on the list of documents.

```
                    Work with Documents in Folders

Folder  . . . ENCK________________________________________
Position to . . . . . .   __________    Starting characters

Type options (and Document), press Enter.
  1=Create      2=Revise       3=Copy         4=Delete         5=View
  6=Print       7=Rename       8=Details      9=Print options  10=Send
  11=Spell      12=File remote 13=Paginate    14=Authority

Opt  Document    Document Description               Revised    Type
__   __________
__   ENCKDOC     Work in progress report            08/14/92   RFTAS400
__   ENCKDOC2    New format WIP report              09/20/92   RFTDCA

                                                                Bottom
F3=Exit     F4=Prompt     F5=Refresh     F10=Search for document
F11=Display names only    F12=Cancel     F13=End search    F24=More keysMIB-II
```

Figure 7-5: Work with Documents in Folders

The remaining portion of the display shows the documents in the folder. The type will show as RFTAS400 for documents that can be revised and as FFTAS400 for documents that cannot be changed. A field appears to the left of each document name that allows you to select an action to be performed on that document:

Option 1 (Create) — Create a document. After specifying document details, you will be placed in the word processor.

Option 2 (Revise) — Invoke the word processor to change the selected document.

Option 3 (Copy) — Create a new document based on the contents of an existing document.

Option 4 (Delete) — Delete the referenced document.

Option 5 (View) — Look at the contents of a document.

Option 6 (Print) — Print a document with the system controlling the format.

Option 7 (Rename) — Change the name of referenced document.

Option 8 (Details) — Change the administrative details associated with a document.

Option 9 (Print opts) — Print a document and control the format.

Option 10 (Send) — Send (mail) a document.

Option 11 (Spell) — Check the spelling in the referenced document.

Option 12 (File remote) — Store the referenced document on another AS/400.

Option 13 (Paginate) — Reset page breaks according to the format of the document.

Option 14 (Authority) — Control who has access to this document.

THE OFFICEVISION/400 WORD PROCESSOR

The standard OfficeVision/400 word processor was designed for use with the 5250 family of workstation. OfficeVision/400 does, however, support two variations of the standard word processor.

If you are using IBM's PC Support program and the PC Support Organizer function is active, you will use the text-assisted word processor, which is similar (but not identical) to the standard word processor. If you are using a foreign terminal type like an IBM 3270 or ASCII display station, you will use the adapted word processor. You can tell if you are using the adapted word processor because the <F24> option will be missing from the Edit display. In the OfficeVision/400 environment, the word processor is normally invoked by the Send Note function or from the Work with Documents in Folders display.

USING THE WORD PROCESSOR

The Edit display for the word processor is composed of a status line at the top, a scale line immediately below the status line, a data entry area below the scale line, and a summary of function key purposes in the lower area. This is shown in Figure 7-6.

```
Insert Text         |                      |   |   |              |Pg 1
NEWDOC,ENCK                                |Typestyle 86 (12p)    |Ln 7
<2...T:...T3...T:...T4...T:...T5...Tv...T6...T:...T7...T:...T8...T:...T9>...:.



_
------------------------------------------------------------------------------
 F1=Copy        F7=Window          F14=Get options        F20=Change formats
 F2=Move        F8=Reset           F15=Columns            F21=Nondisplay keys
 F3=Exit/Save   F9=Instructions    F16=Adjust/Paginate    F22=Spell functions
 F4=Delete      F11=Insert lines   F17=Functions          F23=Word spell aid
 F5=Goto        F12=Cancel         F18=Search/Replace
 F6=Find        F13=Edit options   F19=Print/View
```

Figure 7-6: Word Processor Edit Display

The status line shows the name of the document, the current pitch (characters per inch), the page number (Pg), and line number (Ln) where the cursor is located. If the cursor is on top of a control character, this will also be indicated on the status line.

The scale line shows the settings for the margins and tabs. The left margin is indicated by the < character, the right margin by the > character, and each tab is noted by a T. A v in the scale line shows the center of the line.

Below the scale line is the area for data entry. The word processor automatically enables insert mode, so to enter information into the document simply begin typing. If you are typing a paragraph, the word processor will automatically perform word wrap when you reach the end of a line. To end a paragraph or a line of text, press the <FIELD EXIT> key. A square block will appear at the end of the line or paragraph and the cursor will move to the next line.

You can move around the document by using the arrow keys to move within the displayed area, or the <ROLL UP> and <ROLL DOWN> keys to move forward and backward a screen at a time. If you need to correct the information in a document, you can move the cursor to the area and follow basic guidelines. Other advanced editing tools are available through the use of function keys.

To delete characters, you can use the <BACKSPACE> key to delete the character to the left of the cursor or use the <DELETE> key to delete the character underneath the cursor. To replace characters, make sure insert mode is disabled and simply type over the characters to be changed. To insert characters, make sure insert mode is enabled, and insert the desired characters or codes.

HIGHLIGHTING CHARACTERS

If you want portions of your text to print in bold or underlined type, place control characters before and after the text you want highlighted. These control characters occupy extra space when displayed on the screen but do not occupy any space on the printed output. To insert a control character, hold down the <ALT> key, press the indicated letter key, then release the <ALT> key.

To begin bold type, hold down the <ALT> key, then press B. To end bold type, hold down <ALT>, then press J. To begin underlined type, hold down the <ALT> key, then press U. To end underlined type, hold down <ALT>, then press J.

Note that the <ALT> J sequence is used to terminate both styles of highlighting. If you combine both bold and underlined type, the <ALT> J sequence terminates both highlights. To remove highlighting, delete the control characters in the same fashion you delete normal characters. Make sure you delete both the starting and ending control characters.

SPECIAL FUNCTIONS

OfficeVision/400 makes use of your terminal's function keys to perform block operations, invoke utility functions, perform search and replace operations, and more. In brief, the keys available are:

<F1> — Copy

<F2> — Move

<F3> — Exit/Save

<F4> — Find character

<F5> — Goto

<F6> — Find string

<F7> — Window (adjust view)

<F8> — Reset (terminate find)

<F10> — Instructions

<F11> — Hyphenate

<F12> — Cancel

<F13> — Edit options

<F14> — Get options (open second document)

<F15> — Tables/Columns

<F16> — Adjust/Paginate

<F17> — Functions (merge)

<F18> — Search/Replace

<F19> — Print/View

<F20> — Change format (layout)

<F21> — Nondisplay keys (f-keys on/off)

<F22> — Spell functions

<F23> — Word spell aid

<F24> — More keys

EXITING THE WORD PROCESSOR

When you have completed your additions or changes to the document, press <F3>. The Exit Document menu will then appear. To save the changes to your document, specify Y in the Save document field. If you specify N, all of your changes will be abandoned.

The current name of your document will appear in the Document name field. You can change this name and save the document as a new document. Similarly, you can allow the document to be saved to its default folder or specify a new name in the Folder name field. When you have completed the Exit Document menu, press <ENTER>.

DIRECTORIES/DISTRIBUTION LISTS

Select Option 7 to view and manage distribution information. Available options include:

Option 1 (Personal directories) — Create/maintain your own personal information area.

Option 2 (System directory) — See the user ID and address for each OfficeVision/400 user.

Option 3 (Distribution lists) — Access distribution lists defined within OfficeVision/400.

Option 4 (Nicknames) — Establish a shorter, alternative name for a user ID and address or a distribution list and address.

Option 5 (Search system directory) — Find additional information about a user based on his or her name and/or department.

Option 6 (Departments) — Access information about departments.

DECISION SUPPORT

Option 8 on the OfficeVision/400 opening menu invokes other optional programs. The number and nature of these optional programs can differ from site to site.

ADMINISTRATION

Use Option 9 on the OfficeVision/400 opening menu to manage the administrative information associated with your user ID. If you are the OfficeVision/400 administrator, you will have additional options. Available tasks include:

Option 1 (Change enrollment) — Change your OfficeVision/400 environmental settings.

Option 2 (Display access codes) — Show the access codes that may be assigned to documents to control which departments or individuals may access to them.

Option 3 (Permit others to handle mail/filed documents) — Allow other individuals to access your OfficeVision/400 information.

Option 4 (Work with objects by owner) — Work with the information associated with OfficeVision/400 objects, such as calendars, directories, and folders.

Option 5 (Work with office files) — Save, restore, copy, or delete your calendar and personal directory files.

COMMAND SHORTCUTS

Many of the OfficeVision/400 menus and screen displays can be accessed using command line commands. These commands include:

! **CHKDOC** — Spell check a document

! **CPYDOC** — Copy a document

! **CRTDOC** — Create a document

! **CRTFLR** — Create a folder

! **DSPDOC** — Display a document

! **DSPFLR** — Display a folder

! **EDTDOC** — Edit a document

! **PAGDOC** — Paginate a document

! **PRTDOC** — Print a document

! **RNMDOC** — Rename a document

! **SNDDOC** — Send (mail) a document

! **STRWP** — Start the word processors

! **WRKDOC** — Work with documents in folders

! **WRKFLR** — Work with folders

CHAPTER 8

Data File Utility

DATA FILE UTILITY OVERVIEW

The Data File Utility (DFU) performs operations on data physical files. Operations include changing data within records in files, deleting records from files, and adding records to files.

Indexed or non-indexed physical and logical files can be manipulated with DFU. DFU accesses the external definition of the fields and records in the specified file to determine the file and field format. DFU can create permanent or temporary programs to access the data in a file.

INVOKING DFU

From the Main Menu, invoke DFU by selecting Option 4 (Files, libraries, and folders). After the Data menu appears, select Option 1 (Files). When the Files menu appears, select Option 7 (DFU). From the command line, DFU can be invoked through the Start Data File Utility (STRDFU) command or from the Programmer Menu (STRPGMMNU) command.

START DFU COMMAND

The Start DFU (STRDFU) command uses information from your last DFU session as default values. Other common parameters are OPTION((1 or 2 or 3 or 4 or 5 or *SELECT) (1 or 2)) and FILE(*PRV or <library name/file name>). The Option parameter consists of two parts. The first part allows entries of 1 through 5 and *SELECT. The numbered options correspond to the five DFU Main Menu options, while *SELECT displays the DFU Main Menu. The second part can have a value of 1 to allow updates to the data file or a value of 2 to only display the information in the data file and not allow the information to be changed.

The DFU program parameter allows you to enter the DFU program to be used or to be created. The Library can also be specified if needed. Special value *PRV is the default and is used to specify the previously used value for this parameter.

The Database file parameter contains the name of the data physical file that will be manipulated. The Library can also be specified. Special value *PRV is the default and is used to specify the previously used value for these parameters.

The Member parameter contains the name of the member in the data physical file with which records will be added, changed, or deleted. Special value *PRV is the default and is used to specify the previously used value for these parameters.

The DFU Main Menu will be shown if *SELECT was chosen for the Option prompt with the STRDFU command. The main menu is shown in Figure 8-1.

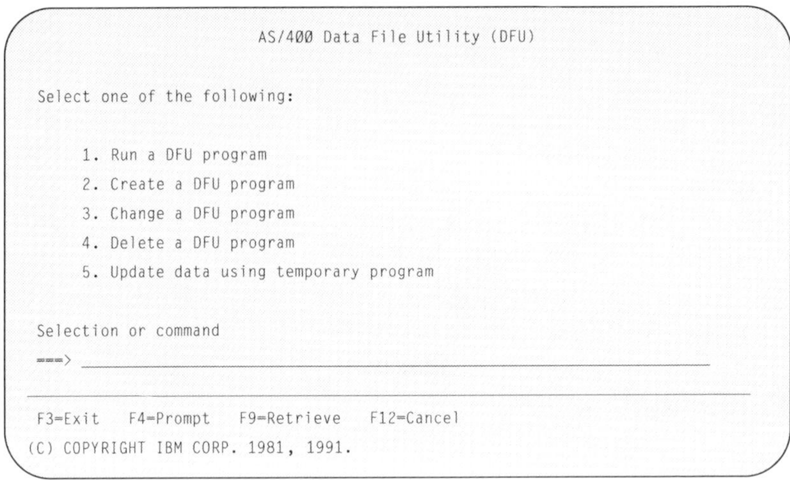

```
                    AS/400 Data File Utility (DFU)

Select one of the following:

     1. Run a DFU program
     2. Create a DFU program
     3. Change a DFU program
     4. Delete a DFU program
     5. Update data using temporary program

Selection or command
===> ____________________________________________

F3=Exit   F4=Prompt   F9=Retrieve   F12=Cancel
(C) COPYRIGHT IBM CORP. 1981, 1991.
```

Figure 8-1: DFU Main Menu

Option 1 runs an existing DFU program. Option 2 creates a new DFU program. Option 3 changes an existing DFU program. Option 4 removes an existing DFU program from the system, and Option 5 creates a temporary program. This program only exists for the duration of your current DFU session.

CREATING A DFU PROGRAM

The Create a DFU Program screen (Figure 8-2) is displayed when a new program is to be created.

```
                      Create a DFU Program

Type choices, press Enter.

  Program . . . . . . . . . .   __________   Name, F4 for list
    Library . . . . . . . . .     *CURLIB___ Name, *CURLIB

  Data file . . . . . . . . .   __________   Name, F4 for list
    Library . . . . . . . . .     *LIBL_____ Name, *LIBL, *CURLIB


F3=Exit      F4=Prompt      F12=Cancel
```

Figure 8-2: Create a DFU Program

Parameters required on this screen are the Program to create and the Library to contain the program. The Data file and Library parameters refer to the file to be accessed by the DFU program. The <F4> key can be used to prompt for these values.

General information needs to be defined for the DFU program. This information is entered through the Define General Information screen shown in Figure 8-3:

```
              Define General Information/Nonindexed File

Type choices, press Enter.

  Job title . . . . . . . . . . . . . . DFUEX01______________________
  Display format  . . . . . . . . . . .   2    1=Single,  2=Multiple
                                               3=Maximum, 4=Row oriented

  Audit report  . . . . . . . . . . . .   Y          Y=Yes, N=No
  S/36 style  . . . . . . . . . . . . .   N          Y=Yes, N=No
  Suppress errors . . . . . . . . . . .   N          Y=Yes, N=No
  Edit numerics . . . . . . . . . . . .   N          Y=Yes, N=No
  Allow updates on roll . . . . . . . .   Y          Y=Yes, N=No
  Record numbers:
    Generate  . . . . . . . . . . . . .   N          Y=Yes, N=No
    Store in a field  . . . . . . . . .   N          Y=Yes, N=No
    Heading . . . . . . . . . . . . . .   *RECNBR_____________
                                          ____________________
                                          ____________________
  Processing  . . . . . . . . . . . . .   2          1=Direct
                                                     2=Sequential

F3=Exit       F12=Cancel        F14=Display definition
```

Figure 8-3: Define General Information

The Job Title parameter contains the string of characters used as a heading and printed on the optional audit report. The Display format parameter determines how fields in the record will be displayed on the screen. DFU can automatically format the screen providing space between each field. Four values are allowed. Value 1 shows one column at a time. Value 2 (the default) shows multiple columns on the screen. DFU determines the spacing between the fields and causes additional screens to be used if needed. Value 3 places the maximum number of fields possible on the screen. And Value 4 places the fields in a row-oriented format.

The Audit report parameter determines if an audit report should be generated. The default is Y, which produces a report. The System/36 style parameter determines if the generated DFU program should operate as System/36 DFU or as native OS/400 DFU. The default is N, producing an OS/400 DFU program.

The Suppress errors parameter can attempt to suppress errors encountered during the program execution. The default is N, which will report errors if they occur. The Edit numerics parameter defines the editing provided for numeric fields. The default of N causes fields to be entered and displayed as a series of digits without numeric editing such as decimal points and commas. An entry of Y causes screens to be displayed allowing edit specification.

The Allow updates on roll parameter determines if records should be updated if fields have been changed and <ROLL UP> or <ROLL DOWN> is pressed. An entry of Y causes DFU to update the changed record and then roll to the next record.

The Work with Record Formats display allows you to select the appropriate record format in the selected data file. Figure 8-4 shows this display.

Option 2 selects record formats for processing while Option 4 removes the record from processing in the DFU program. An entry of Y in the Multiple Records parameter allows display of multiple records on the screen. The Defined parameter indicates if the record format is in use in this DFU program. Individual formats can be selected or <F21> can be used to select all record formats.

```
                         Work with Record Formats

File . . . :   DFUFILE                      Library  . . . . :   ADMIN

Type options, press Enter.  Press F21 to select all.
  2=Specify   4=Delete

Opt  Format       Defined  Description
 _   DFUFILER        N

                                                                  Bottom
F3=Exit                     F5=Refresh           F12=Cancel
F14=Display definition      F21=Select all
```

Figure 8-4: Work with Record Formats

The Select and Sequence Fields display allows selection and sequencing of the fields used in the program. This display is shown in Figure 8-5. This display shows the file, library, and record format names, as well as the field name, description, attributes, length, and type.

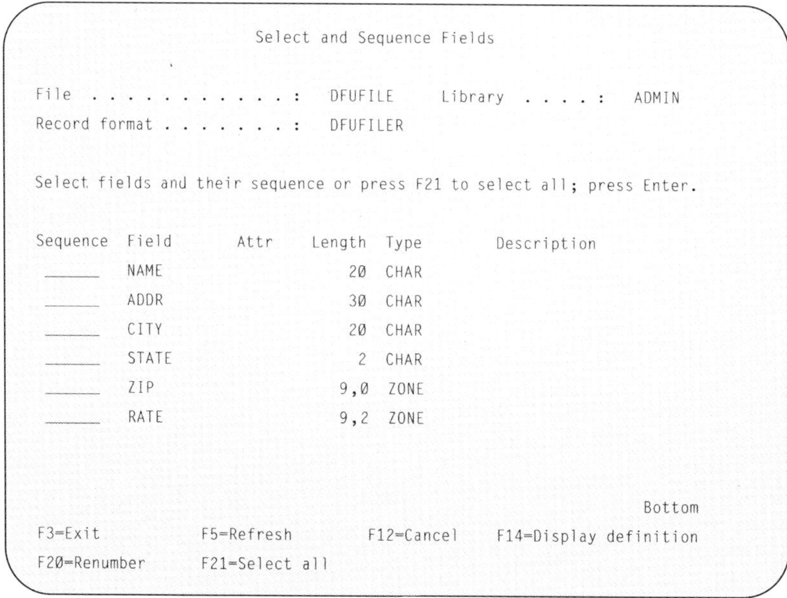

```
                       Select and Sequence Fields

File . . . . . . . . . . . . :   DFUFILE     Library  . . . . :   ADMIN
Record format . . . . . . . :   DFUFILER

Select fields and their sequence or press F21 to select all; press Enter.

Sequence  Field       Attr    Length  Type        Description
 ______   NAME                    20  CHAR
 ______   ADDR                    30  CHAR
 ______   CITY                    20  CHAR
 ______   STATE                    2  CHAR
 ______   ZIP                    9,0  ZONE
 ______   RATE                   9,2  ZONE

                                                              Bottom
F3=Exit          F5=Refresh          F12=Cancel    F14=Display definition
F20=Renumber     F21=Select all
```

Figure 8-5: Select and Sequence Fields

Fields can be selected by specifying a Sequence number that indicates the field's display position. <F21> can be used to select all fields in the order they exist in the file description. Extended field definitions can be specified with the Work with Fields screen. Additional field characteristics can be defined such as accumulation, extended field headings, initial values, validity checks, or edit codes.

The Exit DFU Program Generation display is used to save the program and exit DFU program generation. Additional options include executing the program in either update or browse modes, saving the DDS source created for the program displays, specifying the public authority granted, or specifying the descriptive text for the program.

RUNNING A DFU PROGRAM

A DFU program can be executed with the Start DFU (STRDFU) or Change Data (CHGDTA) commands from the DFU Main Menu or from the Exit DFU Program Definition screen. The Change a Data File screen is displayed to execute the program. This display is shown in Figure 8-6:

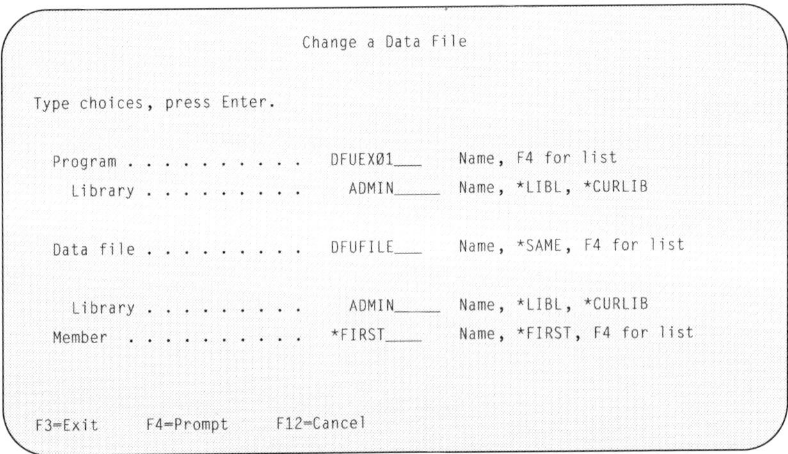

Change a Data File
Type choices, press Enter.
Program . . . . DFUEX01___ Name, F4 for list
Library . . . . ADMIN_____ Name, *LIBL, *CURLIB
Data file . . . . DFUFILE___ Name, *SAME, F4 for list
Library . . . . ADMIN_____ Name, *LIBL, *CURLIB
Member . . . . *FIRST____ Name, *FIRST, F4 for list
F3=Exit F4=Prompt F12=Cancel

Figure 8-6: Change a Data File

Some parameters will default to *PRV, indicating the values for the previous execution will be used. The name of the DFU Program identifies the name of the program to be executed and is required. The Data file parameter indicates the name of the data file to be used by the program, as well as the library and member. The initial program mode will be in entry mode if the file is empty and in change mode if records exist.

ADDING NEW RECORDS

The following example screen (Figure 8-7) shows the entry mode display:

```
DFUEX01                                           Mode . . . . :   ENTRY
Format . . . . :   DFUFILER__                     File . . . . :   DFUFILE

NAME:     ____________________
ADDR:     ______________________________
CITY:     ____________________
STATE:    __
ZIP:      _________
RATE:     _________


F3=Exit                  F5=Refresh                F6=Select format
F9=Insert                F10=Entry                 F11=Change
```

Figure 8-7: Entry Mode

Unless initial values were established when the program was created, numeric fields will contain zeros and alphanumeric fields will contain blanks. Available function keys are:

<F3> — Exits record addition

<F5> — Refreshes the screen

<F6> — Displays a record format list to select a format

<F9> — Inserts a new record at the current position

<F10> — Changes to entry mode

<F11> — Changes to change mode

Records will be entered to the end of the file. A new screen will be displayed with the fields initialized to appropriate values depending on type, or to initial values.

CHANGING RECORDS IN A FILE

Records can be changed when the program is in change mode. Indexed file records are accessed by entering a key value, while sequential file records are presented in execution order.

The change mode display is the same as the entry mode with the exception that the fields contain the record information. Pressing <ENTER> after changing information updates the record.

Additional function keys available in change mode are:

<F17> — Displays the values in batch accumulator fields

<F21> — Displays the program execution status

INSERTING RECORDS

Records are inserted into the file at the current position with the <F9> key. The program will be placed in entry mode, with all entry mode characteristics in force.

DELETING RECORDS

Records are be deleted from the file with the <F23> key. The program must be in change mode, and the record at the current position will be deleted. Confirmation is required to delete a record.

SAVING AND EXITING

Pressing <F3> in entry or change mode shows the End Data Entry display. This display shows the number of records processed and indicates the number of records added, changed, and deleted. A screen will be displayed showing the batch accumulators if accumulation was selected during program generation. The optional audit trail report will be printed when DFU is exited. An example audit trail report is shown in Figure 8-8.

```
                     Display Spooled File
File . . . . . :   QPDZDTALOG                       Page/Line   1/1
Control . . . . .  ______                           Columns     1 - 78
Find . . . . . .   ______________________________
*...+....1....+....2....+....3....+....4....+....5....+....6....+....7....+...
 5738SS1     V2R1M1  920306                             AUDIT LOG
  Library/File . . . . .    ADMIN/DFUFILE
  Member . . . . . . . .    DFUFILE
  Job Title  . . . . . .    DFUEX01
                    *RECNBR   NAME                 ADDR
 Changed                  1   MICHAEL RYAN         123 MAIN STREET
                              MICHAEL J. RYAN
                    RATE
                       4.95
Batch accumulators are displayed
     RATE                              .00
Total accumulators are displayed
     RATE                              .00
                     0  Records Added
                     1  Records Changed
                     0  Records Deleted
                                                                 More...
F3=Exit   F12=Cancel   F19=Left   F20=Right   F24=More keys
```

Figure 8-8: Audit Trail Report

CHANGING DATA WITH A TEMPORARY DFU PROGRAM

Data can be changed with a temporary program. The Update Data Using Temporary Program display is shown in Figure 8-9:

```
                  Update Data Using Temporary Program

Type choices, press Enter.

  Data file . . . . . . . . .   DFUFILE___     Name, F4 for list
    Library . . . . . . . . .     ADMIN_____   Name, *LIBL, *CURLIB
  Member  . . . . . . . . . .   DFUFILE___     Name, *FIRST, F4 for list


F3=Exit     F4=Prompt     F12=Cancel
```

Figure 8-9: Update Data with Temporary Program

This screen requires the name of the data file, library, and member to be accessed. You can prompt for these values with the <F4> key. The temporary DFU program automatically selects all record formats and all fields. Defaults are taken for the Define general information and audit control parameters. These defaults produce a multiple column display format with all added, changed, and deleted records printed at end of job.

All standard operations are available with a temporary program, such as adding records through entry mode and changing and deleting records through change mode. The normal End Data Entry screen is displayed when you press the <F3> key.

CHAPTER 9

Screen Design Aid

SCREEN DESIGN AID OVERVIEW

The Screen Design Aid (SDA) creates, modifies, and tests display files and menus. SDA is an interactive method for creating the Data Description Specifications (DDS) for a display file or menu. Display files are the interface between a program and the user. Menus provide a method of choosing programs or commands to execute. Display files (a file with the DSPF attribute) and menus (an object of type MNU) are described using DDS.

SDA provides the capability to manipulate the DDS interactively, allowing you to see the screen as it is being created or revised, and to move and position the fields and constants. All display file attributes, including attributes such as bold and mandatory entry, are available for selection through SDA.

INVOKING SDA

From the Main Menu, invoke SDA by selecting Option 5 (Programming). After the Program menu appears, select Option 3 (Utilities). When the CMDSTR menu appears, select Option 66 (Start Screen Design Aid). From the command line, SDA can be invoked through the Start Screen Design Aid (STRSDA) command or from the Programmer Menu (STRPGMMNU command).

The STRSDA command uses information from your last SDA session as default values. Other common parameters are SRCFILE(*PRV or <library name/file name>) SRCMBR(*PRV or <member name>) and OPTION(1 or 2 or 3 or *SELECT).

Command default values are *SELECT for the SDA option parameter and *PRV (for previous) for the Source file, Library, and Member parameters. The member contains the DDS for the record formats. Each member can have multiple record formats, with each format containing the DDS statements for screen or portion of a screen.

Figure 9-1 will be displayed if the SDA option parameter value was *SELECT.

```
                    AS/400 Screen Design Aid (SDA)

 Select one of the following:

      1. Design screens
      2. Design menus
      3. Test display files

 Selection or command
 ===> ____________________________________________________________

 F1=Help   F3=Exit   F4=Prompt   F9=Retrieve   F12=Cancel
 (C) COPYRIGHT IBM CORP. 1981, 1991.
```

Figure 9-1: SDA Main Menu

Option 1 creates and updates display files, Option 2 creates and updates menus, and Option 3 tests existing display files.

DESIGNING SCREENS

The Work with Display Records screen shows the records that are contained within the selected member, file, and library. Figure 9-2 is an example of the Work with Display Records screen:

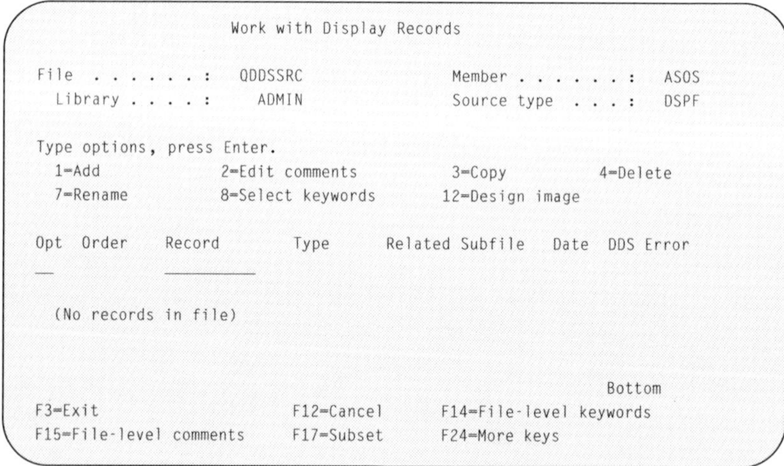

```
                     Work with Display Records

 File . . . . . . :   QDDSSRC          Member . . . . . . :   ASOS
   Library . . . . :    ADMIN          Source type  . . . :   DSPF

 Type options, press Enter.
   1=Add            2=Edit comments      3=Copy          4=Delete
   7=Rename         8=Select keywords   12=Design image

 Opt  Order    Record        Type     Related Subfile   Date  DDS Error
 __            _________

   (No records in file)

                                                             Bottom
 F3=Exit                     F12=Cancel      F14=File-level keywords
 F15=File-level comments     F17=Subset      F24=More keys
```

Figure 9-2: Work with Display Records

Available options with the Work with Display Records display are:

Option 1 — Adds a new record.

Option 2 — Edits comments associated with the record.

Option 3 — Copies an existing display record to a new record name.

Option 4 — Removes an existing display record from the member.

Option 7 — Renames an existing display record.

Option 8 — Selects DDS keywords for the display record.

Option 12 — Designs an image by changing an existing display record.

The function keys used on this display include the standard function keys with the addition of:

<F11> — Displays the text associated with the member

<F14> — Changes the file-level DDS keywords for the member

<F15> — Changes the file-level comments

<F17> — Subsets the list of display records

Selecting Option 1 causes the following display (Figure 9-3) to be shown:

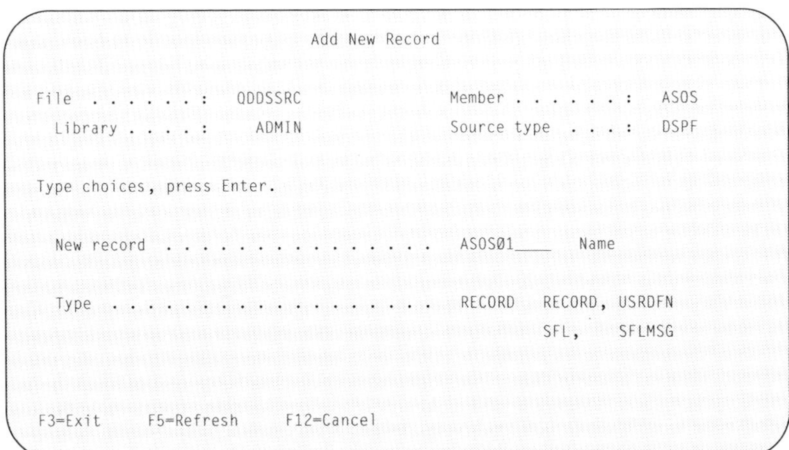

Figure 9-3: Add New Record

Values must be specified values for the name of the new record and the type of record. Record is the name of the display record in the member and record type is the type of the record in the member. Valid record types are:

RECORD — A display record (most common)

USRDFN — A user-defined display record

SFL — A subfile record

SFLMSG — A subfile message record

SFLCTL — A subfile control record

Manipulating a Record Format

A blank screen appears when creating a new record format, while the screen image appears when changing an existing format. The screen is a design area where fields and constants are positioned and attributes assigned. Fields and constants are specified with format characters to indicate the data type, size, and display characteristics. This information is converted into DDS by SDA.

Function keys available when designing a screen include:

<F3> — Ends screen design and proceeds to the Exit Design Image screen.

<F4> — Shows the Work with Fields display for attribute selection.

<F6> — Shows the Condition Work Screen display for specifying indicators that condition record display for the design process.

<F9> — Provides for selection of additional records to be shown on the display in the design process.

<F10> — Shows the Select Database Files display to select a file from which you can copy field definitions.

<F11> — Displays the list of database fields on the bottom row of the screen. This key is a toggle; press <F11> again to remove the list.

<F12> — Saves the work and returns to the Work with Display Records display.

<F14> — Displays a horizontal and vertical ruler. This key is a toggle; press <F14> again to remove the ruler.

<F15> — Prompts for subfile information.

<F17> — Prints the contents of the Design Image screen.

<F18> — Moves the cursor to the attribute position of the next field.

<F19> — Moves the cursor to the attribute position of the previous field.

<F20> — Displays the constants in reverse image.

<F21> — Displays additional selected records on the screen. This key is a toggle; pressing <F21> again will remove the additional records from the display.

ADDING AND DELETING FIELDS AND CONSTANTS

Fields and constants are added by specifying format and attribute codes on the design screen. Each field or constant must be separated by at least one blank space, and no fields or constants can be placed in row 1, column 1 of a display file. A field can be placed directly after another field or constant (including the intervening space) by entering the format character over the last character position of the previous field or constant. A constant can be entered by ending the constant with a double quotation mark and beginning the new constant or field.

Fields are added by entering a plus sign followed by the format code for the field type desired. The format codes for different field types are:

I — Input only field; alphanumeric

O — Output only field; alphanumeric

B — Both input and output (update) field; alphanumeric

3 — Input only field; numeric

6 — Output only field; numeric

9 — Both input and output (update) field; numeric

Floating point fields are added by specifying the appropriate numeric format codes followed by an E for single precision or a D for double precision.

The length of a field is determined by specifying format characters for each character in the length of the field or by specifying the format character followed by the length of the field in parentheses.

Constants are added by typing the constant onto the design screen in the position desired. Constants are ended with a blank character. A constant that consists of several words can be defined as a single constant by placing single quotation marks around the group of words. A single constant can be redefined from several words on the screen by placing quotation marks around the words. System-defined constants can be placed in any valid location on the display screen. These predefined constants are:

***DATE** — Provides the system date.

***TIME** — Provides the system time.

***USER** — Provides the current user name.

***SYSNAME** — Provides the system name.

Fields and constants can be deleted from the display screen by spacing over the entire field, including immediately preceding position (the attribute byte) or by placing the character D in the position immediately preceding the field or constant and pressing <ENTER>.

Figure 9-4 shows fields and constants being added to and deleted from the display screen:

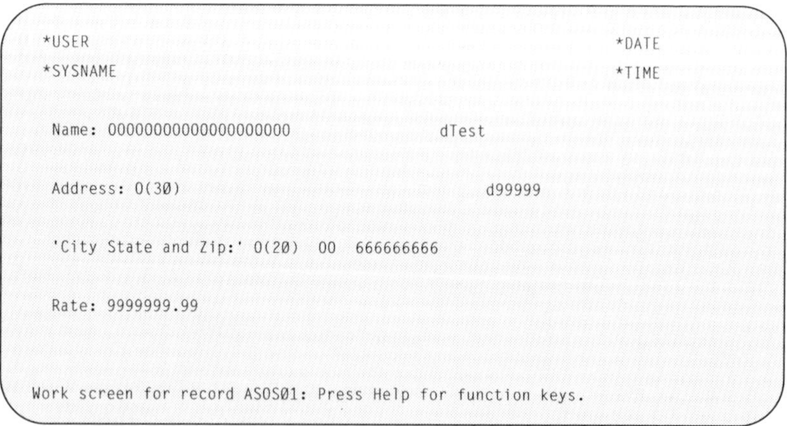

*USER
*DATE
*SYSNAME
*TIME
Name: 00000000000000000000
dTest
Address: 0(30)
d99999
'City State and Zip:' 0(20) 00 666666666
Rate: 9999999.99
Work screen for record ASOS01: Press Help for function keys.

Figure 9-4: Fields and Constants Being Added and Deleted

SPECIFYING ATTRIBUTES AND COLOR

Attributes, including color, can be specified for fields and attributes. The attribute codes are placed in the character position immediately preceding the field or constant.

The following is a list of attribute codes:

B — Blink

H — High intensity

N — Nondisplay

R — Reverse image

S — Column separators

U — Underline

CB — Color blue

CG — Color green

CP — Color pink

CR — Color red

CT — Color turquoise

CW — Color white

Attributes are removed by placing a minus sign and the attribute code in the attribute position of the field or constant. -A removes all attributes and -CA removes all colors. The following example screen (Figure 9-5) shows adding attributes and colors to fields and constants.

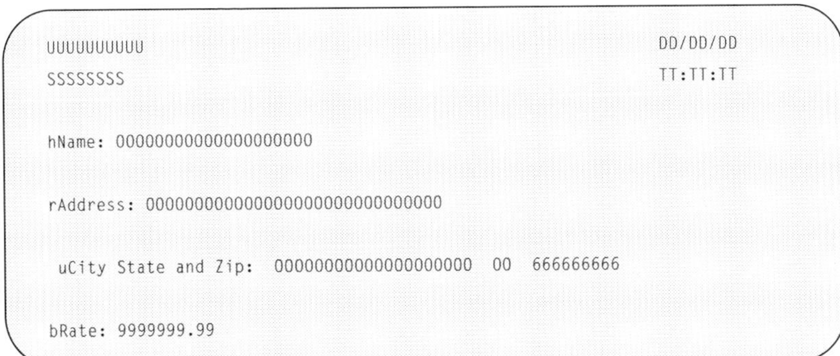

UUUUUUUUUU
DD/DD/DD
SSSSSSSS
TT:TT:TT
hName: 0000000000000000000
rAddress: 000000000000000000000000000000
uCity State and Zip: 0000000000000000000 00 666666666
bRate: 9999999.99

Figure 9-5: Adding Attributes

Attributes can also be added by placing an asterisk in the attribute byte and pressing <ENTER>. This shows the Extended Field Definition display allowing entry of attributes. A question mark in the attribute position shows the field length, type, and field name. The field can be renamed with this method.

CHANGING THE POSITION OF FIELDS AND CONSTANTS

Fields and constants can be moved, copied, shifted, and centered with SDA commands. Place the position commands in the attribute position of the field or constant and pressing <ENTER>. Multiple fields or constants can be changed with one operation. Block positioning can also be used to position several fields and constants.

The AC command centers a field or constant in the same row. A field or constant is moved by specifying a minus sign in the attribute byte of the field to be moved and an equal sign at the target position. A field is copied by specifying a minus sign in the attribute position of the field to be copied and a double equal sign at the target position.

Blocks of fields and constants can be moved or copied by specifying a minus sign in the upper left corner of the block and a minus sign in the lower right corner of the block. Specify one equal sign (for a move) or two equal signs (for a copy) in the target position for the block.

Fields and constants are shifted using the < and > characters. Shift left by placing the < characters in the attribute position. This shifts the field or constant to the left the number of < characters. Shift right by placing the > characters in the attribute position. This shifts the field or constant to the right the number of < characters.

A message is displayed if an error is made changing the position of fields and constants, possibly by moving or creating a field over another field. Pressing <ENTER> clears the error message and restores the design screen to the state it was in before the invalid operation.

ADDING FIELDS FROM A DATABASE FILE

Database files containing fields to be added to the SDA design screen are selected with the Select Database Files display. SDA will then create a list of fields and allow positioning of the fields on the design screen. The fields have the same definition as their definition in the file. The Select Database Files display is accessed by with <F10> and is shown in Figure 9-6.

```
                    Select Database Files

Type options and names, press Enter.
  1=Display database field list
  2=Select all fields for input (I)
  3=Select all fields for output (O)
  4=Select all fields for both (B) input and output

Option    Database File   Library      Record
  1         DFUFILE___     ADMIN_____   DFUFILER__
  _         __________     __________   __________
  _         __________     __________   __________
  _         __________     __________   __________

F3=Exit     F4=Prompt     F12=Cancel
```

Figure 9-6: Select Database Files

Identify the database file, library, and record format name (if needed). The <F4> key can be used to prompt for these values. Four options are available for selecting fields. Option 1 provides a list of the fields in the database file. Option 2 selects all fields as input fields. Option 3 selects all fields as output fields. Option 4 selects all fields as input and output fields. An example database field list is shown in Figure 9-7.

```
                    Select Database Fields

Record . . . :   DFUFILER

Type information, press Enter.
  Number of fields to roll . . . . . . . . . . . . . . . . . .      8
  Name of field to search for . . . . . . . . . . . . . . .   __________

Type options, press Enter.
  1=Display extended field description
  2=Select for input (I), 3=Select for output (O), 4=Select for both (B)

Option  Field       Length   Type   Column Heading
  3     NAME          20      A     NAME
  3     ADDR          30      A     ADDR
  3     CITY          20      A     CITY
  3     STATE          2      A     STATE
  3     ZIP          9,0      S     ZIP
  4     RATE         9,2      S     RATE

                                                          Bottom
F3=Exit   F12=Cancel
```

Figure 9-7: Database Field List

You can use the <ROLL UP> and <ROLL DOWN> keys to page through the field list. There are four options to select fields, and fields can be selected as different types. Option 1 provides an extended description. Option 2 selects the field as an input field. Option 3 selects the field as an output field. Option 4 selects the field as an input/output field. Selected fields are shown on the bottom of the design screen. Positioning codes are placed on the design screen at the position where the fields should be located.

The ampersand is the special character for positioning. Other characters are used to indicate if column headings (from the database file) should be brought onto the screen. Multiple fields are specified by adding a number following the special character to indicate the correct field. The following summarizes the special characters:

& or &n — Positions the database field but does not add the column heading.

&C or &nC — Positions the database field and centers the column heading above the field.

&L or &nL — Positions the database field and adds the column heading to the left of the field.

&R or &nR — Positions the database field and adds the column heading to the right of the field.

&P or &nP — Positions the column heading only.

SAVING AND EXITING

The <F12> key saves the current record format and returns to the Work with Display Records screen. The <F3> exit key shows the exit SDA Work Screen display where you can save the changes, exit without saving, or return to the design screen.

Exiting the Work with Display Records or Exit SDA Work Screen displays causes the Save DDS-Create Display File screen to be shown. This display is shown in Figure 9-8. The default options will save the DDS, submit a Create Display File (CRTDSPF) command in batch, and exit SDA.

```
                    Save DDS - Create Display File

Type choices, press Enter.

  Save DDS source . . . . . . . . . . . . . .  Y             Y=Yes
    Source file . . . . . . . . . . . . . . .  QDDSSRC___    F4 for list
      Library . . . . . . . . . . . . . . . .  ADMIN_____    Name, *LIBL ...
    Member . . . . . . . . . . . . . . . . . . ASOS______    F4 for list
    Text . . . . . . . . . . . . . . . . . . . ____________________________

  Create display file . . . . . . . . . . . .  Y             Y=Yes
    Prompt for parameters . . . . . . . . . .  _             Y=Yes
    Display file . . . . . . . . . . . . . . . ASOS______    F4 for list
      Library . . . . . . . . . . . . . . . .  ADMIN_____    Name, *CURLIB
    Replace existing file . . . . . . . . . .  _             Y=Yes

  Submit create job in batch . . . . . . . .   Y             Y=Yes

  Specify additional
    save or create options . . . . . . . . .   _             Y=Yes

F3=Exit   F4=Prompt   F12=Cancel
```

Figure 9-8: Save DDS-Create Display

The first parameter, Save DDS source, defaults to Y if any changes have been made to the member. The Member, Source file, and Library parameters specify the location to save the member. The <F4> key can be used to prompt for these values. The Text parameter specifies the text description associated with this member. The Create display file prompt determines if SDA should execute the CRTDSPF command to create a display file from the DDS. The Prompt for parameters option prompts the CRTDSPF command to specify additional create options.

The Display file prompt identifies the name of the display file and defaults to the name of the member. The Replace existing file prompt causes SDA to overwrite an existing member when saved. The Submit create job in batch prompt defaults to Y and determines if SDA should submit the CRTDSPF command to batch. The Specify additional save or create options provides options resequence the member and specify a job description for the batch creation of the display file.

CREATING A MENU

A menu consists of a display screen containing the menu text (an object of type MNUDDS) and an associated file that contains the commands to be executed (an object of type MNUCMD). Menus are created in a similar manner to display files. The menu display file name can be any valid name. The menu command file is automatically named menunameQQ.

Option 2, Design Menus, from the SDA Main Menu shows a display requiring values for a Source file and Library name and a Menuname. The <F4> key can be used to prompt for these values. The Specify Menu Options screen will then be displayed. This screen requires a value for the Work with menu image and commands prompt (usually Y). This allows entry of the menu text and the associated menu commands.

As with display file, creating a new menu causes a blank screen to be displayed while revising an existing menu causes the selected menu to be displayed. An example new menu screen is shown below in Figure 9-9:

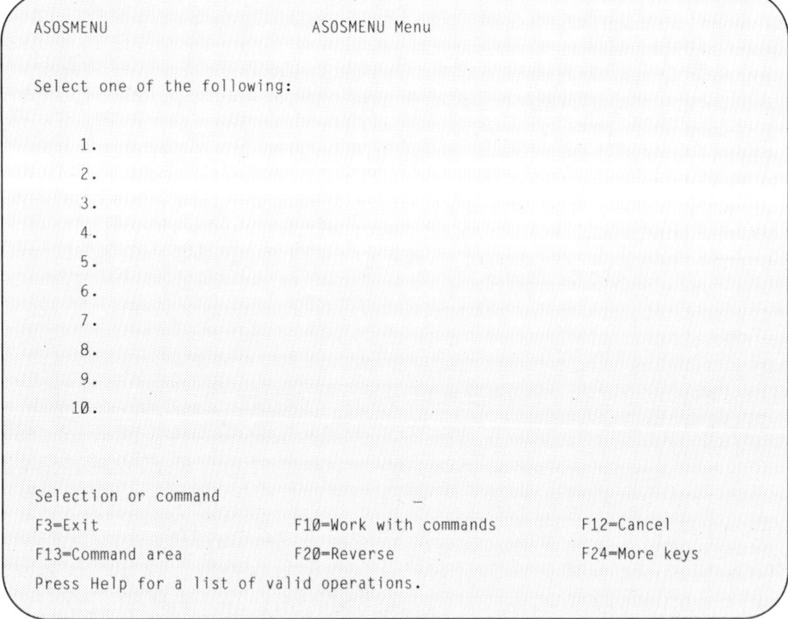

ASOSMENU
ASOSMENU Menu
Select one of the following:
1.
2.
3.
4.
5.
6.
7.
8.
9.
10.
Selection or command
F3=Exit
F10=Work with commands
F12=Cancel
F13=Command area
F20=Reverse
F24=More keys
Press Help for a list of valid operations.

Figure 9-9: New Menu

The supplied option numbers can be used or a free format menu can be created. Option numbers in either case must be in the range of 1-99. The default format has the menu name in the upper left corner of the screen, the "menuname Menu" title centered over the menu options, and the subsequent lines (3-20) used for menu options.

ENTERING MENU TEXT

Command text is entered as with designing a screen including format characters, attribute codes, and method of changing the positions are the same. Menu text lines are constants. System supplied predefined constants can also be used. Attributes are added to constants in the same fashion as with designing a screen.

The following example screen (Figure 9-10) is a menu with the text for several options completed.

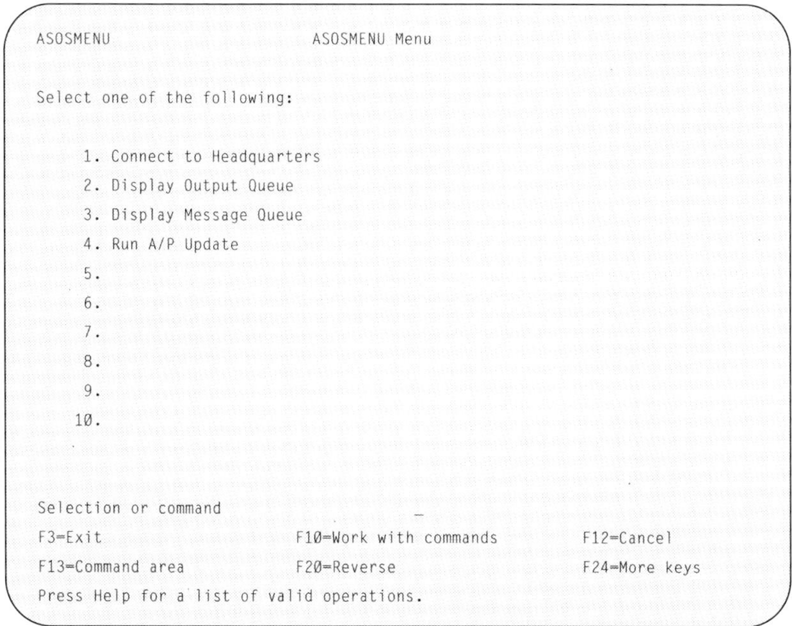

Figure 9-10: Menu with Option Text

<F13> is used to work with the command area, which is the area at the bottom of the screen where menu option and commands are entered. The default text for the command line is Selection or command. Change the default by overtyping the text. The location of the command line is determined by the Create Menu (CRTMNU) options chosen.

ENTERING MENU COMMANDS

<F10> displays the Define Menu Commands screen, as shown in Figure 9-11. This display contains the command to be executed when the corresponding menu option is selected. A maximum of 99 commands can be defined, each relating to a specific menu option.

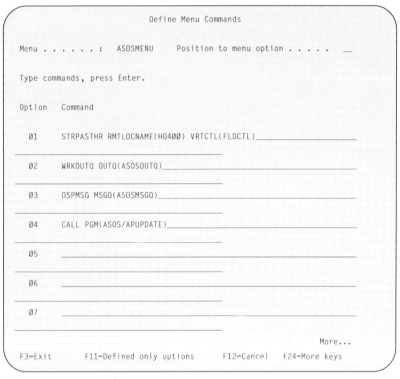

```
                          Define Menu Commands

 Menu . . . . . . :    ASOSMENU      Position to menu option . . . . .  _

 Type commands, press Enter.

 Option   Command

   01     STRPASTHR RMTLOCNAME(HQ400) VRTCTL(FLDCTL)

   02     WRKOUTQ OUTQ(ASOSOUTQ)

   03     DSPMSG MSGQ(ASOSMSGQ)

   04     CALL PGM(ASOS/APUPDATE)

   05

   06

   07
                                                                  More...
 F3=Exit      F11=Defined only options       F12=Cancel   F24=More keys
```

Figure 9-11: Define Menu Commands

The Position to menu option prompt allows you to position the list to a certain menu option. A menu option number, or a plus or minus sign, can be used for navigation. The <F11> key only displays menu options that have been already defined.

Next to each option number is a command line. Enter the command associated with the menu option. The <F4> key can be used to prompt the command to provide the appropriate command parameters. Placing a question mark in front of the command provides command prompting when the menu option is selected.

SAVING AND EXITING

Pressing <F3> will exit the Define Commands screen. Pressing <F3> at the Menu Options display will proceed to the Exit SDA Menus screen. The following example screen (Figure 9-12) shows the Exit SDA Menus display:

```
                         Exit SDA Menus

 File . . . . . . :   QDDSSRC       DDS member . . . . . :   ASOSMENU
   Library . . . . :    ADMIN       Commands member . . . :   ASOSMENUQQ

 Type choices, press Enter.

   Save new or updated menu source . . Y          Y=Yes, N=No
     For choice Y=Yes:
       Source file . . . . . . . . . . QDDSSRC___  Name, 4 for list
         Library . . . . . . . . . . . ADMIN_____  Name, *LIBL, *CURLIB
       Text . . . . . . . . . . . . . . __________________________________
       Replace menu members . . . . . . Y          Y=Yes, N=No

   Create menu objects  . . . . . . . . Y          Y=Yes, N=No
     For choice Y=Yes:
       Prompt for parameters  . . . . . N          Y=Yes, N=No
       Object library . . . . . . . . . ADMIN_____ Name, *CURLIB
       Replace menu objects . . . . . . Y          Y=Yes, N=No

 F3=Exit     F4=Prompt     F12=Cancel
```

Figure 9-12: Exit SDA Menus

Values for the file and library of the DDS member and the commands member are displayed. The DDS member contains the DDS statements for the menu and the commands member contains the commands for the menu options.

The Save new or updated menu source parameter defaults to Y if changes have been made to the member. This response requires entries for the Source file and Library parameters identifying the location for the source statements. The <F4> key can be used to prompt for these values.

The Text parameter is a text description associated with this member. The Replace menu members prompt defaults to Y if changes have been made to the member. The Create menu objects prompt defaults to Y if any changes have been made to the member. A response of Y requires entries for the following prompts.

The Prompt for parameters displays the prompted Create Menu (CRTMNU) command allowing entry of menu creation parameters such as CMDLINE and DSPKEYS. The CRTMNU CMDLINE parameter determines the type of command line. The CMDLINE parameter can have one of three values. *LONG is a command line that begins on line 19 and is two lines long. *SHORT is a command line that begins on line 20 and is one line long. And *NONE is no command line.

The DSPKEYS parameter determines if the function key legend is shown at the bottom of the screen. The DSPKEYS parameter can have one of two values: *YES, which displays the function key legend, or *NO, which does not display the function key legend.

The Object library prompt identifies the library for the new menu objects. The Replace menu objects prompt defaults to Y if the member is to be changed. The menu is created interactively. A status message is sent when the creation is complete.

CHAPTER 10

Programming Development Manager

PROGRAMMING DEVELOPMENT MANAGER OVERVIEW

The Programming Development Manager (PDM) is a list-oriented interface for working with different objects, including libraries and members in a file. PDM allows access to the Source Entry Utility (SEU), the Data File Utility (DFU), and the Screen Design Aid (SDA) through the list interface. PDM also provides a user-defined option mechanism where your own commands and IBM system commands can be used on the objects in the list.

PDM furnishes a grouping technique that allows you to subset a list of objects. PDM also uses a command structure that allows you to perform operations without needing to know the intricacies of the command. PDM uses information from the selected object (name or object type, for example) to complete the command parameters.

INVOKING PDM

From the Main Menu, invoke PDM by selecting Option 5 (Programming). After the Program menu appears, select Option 2 (Programming Development Manager (PDM). From the command line, PDM can be invoked through the Start PDM (STRPDM) command. Figure 10-1 will be displayed when the STRPDM command is executed:

```
                AS/400 Programming Development Manager (PDM)

Select one of the following:

     1. Work with libraries
     2. Work with objects
     3. Work with members

     9. Work with user-defined options


Selection or command
===> ____________________________________________________________________
--------------------------------------------------------------------------
F3=Exit        F4=Prompt        F9=Retrieve        F10=Command entry
F12=Cancel     F18=Change defaults
```

Figure 10-1: STRPDM

Option 1 executes the Work with Libraries using PDM (WRKLIBPDM) command. Option 2 runs the Work with Objects using PDM (WRKOBJPDM) command. Option 3 executes the Work with Members using PDM (WRKMBRPDM) command. Option 9 changes the user-defined options associated with PDM.

PDM provides common actions, functions, and a common interface across the four PDM selections. The common actions are accessed through the use of options selected from the list-oriented interface. The common functions are accomplished through the use of standard, common, and specific function keys. The common interface is a list-oriented interface that displays the objects to be accessed in a list.

THE LIST-ORIENTED INTERFACE

The list-oriented interface of PDM provides a common method of accessing objects. An example of this interface is shown in Figure 10-2:

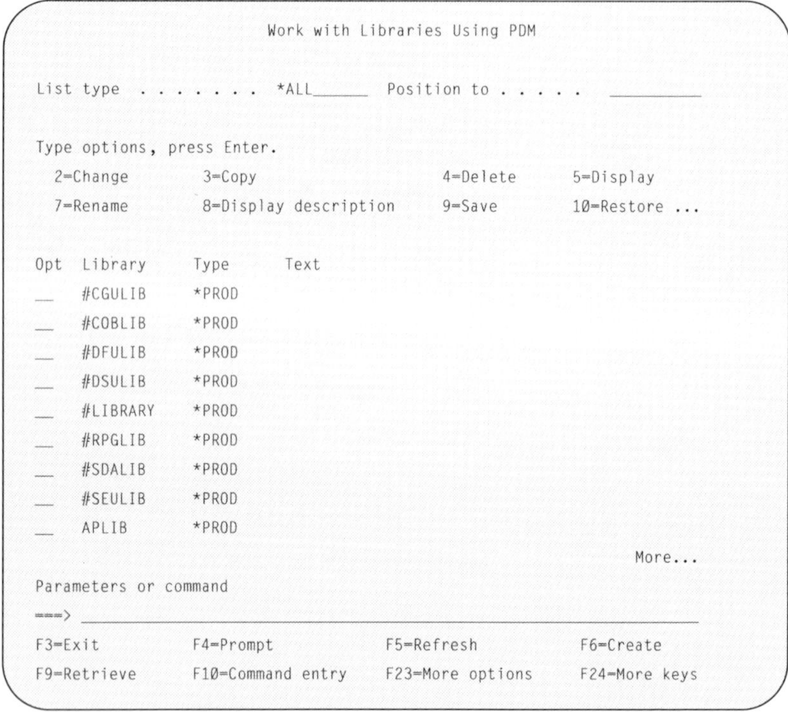

Work with Libraries Using PDM
List type . . . . *ALL______ Position to . . . . . __________
Type options, press Enter.
2=Change 3=Copy 4=Delete 5=Display
7=Rename 8=Display description 9=Save 10=Restore ...
Opt Library Type Text
__ #CGULIB *PROD
__ #COBLIB *PROD
__ #DFULIB *PROD
__ #DSULIB *PROD
__ #LIBRARY *PROD
__ #RPGLIB *PROD
__ #SDALIB *PROD
__ #SEULIB *PROD
__ APLIB *PROD
More...
Parameters or command
===> ____
F3=Exit F4=Prompt F5=Refresh F6=Create
F9=Retrieve F10=Command entry F23=More options F24=More keys

Figure 10-2: List-Oriented Interface

Several common points exist in this interface, regardless of the type of object being accessed. The library containing the objects is shown, an entry field for positioning the list is provided, lists of the allowable options and function keys are shown, and the objects are displayed in a column with the type and text description of the object.

An Option area is provided for each object in the list. Multiple options can be selected for objects in the list. The actions to be performed by the option selected will be performed on each object in sequence, from the top to the bottom of the list.

SUBSETTING A LIST

The <F17> key subsets the list of displayed objects. A display is shown containing the appropriate selection criteria for the type of object being accessed. Any of the criteria can be used for subsetting the list. The special value *ALL can be used to have PDM accept any value for the entry.

The Work with Libraries using PDM (WRKLIBPDM) subsetting criteria are:

The name of the library — A specific name, a generic name, or *ALL.

The library type — *TEST, *PROD, or *ALL.

The text description — A specific description or *ALL.

The Work with Objects using PDM (WRKOBJPDM) subsetting criteria is:

The name of the object — A specific name, a generic name, or *ALL.

The object type — A specific type (in the form *type) or *ALL.

The object attribute — A specific attribute name, a generic attribute name, the special value *BLANK (meaning no attribute) or *ALL.

The text description — A specific description or *ALL.

The Work with Members using PDM (WRKMBRPDM) subsetting criteria is:

The name of the member — A specific name, a generic name, or "*ALL".

The member type — A specific type name, a generic type name, the special value *BLANK (meaning no type), or *ALL.

The earliest date — Last modified to include (which defaults to 01/01/00).

The latest date — Last modified to include (which defaults to 12/31/99).

The text description — A specific description or *ALL.

FUNCTION KEYS

Three types of function keys are used in PDM: standard function keys, common function keys, and specific function keys. Standard function keys are those used with most OS/400 commands. Common function keys are specific to PDM but provide common function. Specific function keys are ones that are only appropriate for a specific PDM selection.

The standard function keys available from within PDM are:

<F1> (or the <HELP> key) — Provides general or context-sensitive help.

<F3> — Exits PDM or stops a function with no action taken.

<F4> — Prompts a command entered on the command line.

<F5> — Refreshes the screen and rebuilds the list. <F5> restores the list to its original contents.

<F9> — Retrieves a previously entered command from the command line.

<F12> — Cancels the current function and return to the previous display.

<F23> — Displays the options not currently displayed on the screen.

<F24> — Displays the function keys not currently displayed on the screen.

Function keys that are common to PDM selections include:

<F4> — Prompts the command associated with the option and places any available information (from the list entry) in the appropriate keywords for the command.

<F6> — Creates a new object based on the type of object being accessed.

<F10> — Displays the Command Entry screen.

<F11> — Changes the information displayed in the list. <F11> is a toggle key, meaning the display changes between a multiple column display of object names only or a display of a single column list of names, types, and text descriptions.

<F13> — Repeats the action performed by an option entered in a previous list entry. The action is performed for all the remaining entries in a list for which the option is valid.

<F16> — Displays the Work with User-Defined Options screen.

<F17> — Subsets the list being displayed.

<F18> — Changes the defaults associated with the PDM session.

<F21> — Prints the current list of objects.

An example of a specific function key for the Work with Libraries using PDM (WRKLIBPDM) command is <F6>, which executes the Create Library (CRTLIB) command to create a new library, or adds an entry to a library list.

Specific function keys for the Work with Objects using PDM (WRKOBJPDM) command are:

<F6> — Displays the Create Commands menu (GO CMDCRT) to allow you to select the appropriate command for creating a new object.

<F14> — Displays the size or the attribute of the object. <F14> is a toggle key, meaning either the sizes or the attributes of the objects in the list will be displayed.

Specific function keys for the Work with Members using PDM (WRKMBRPDM) command are:

<F6> — Invokes SEU to allow you to create a new source member.

<F14> — Displays the date or the type of the member. <F14> is a toggle key, meaning either the dates or the types of the members in the list will be displayed.

<F15> — Sorts the display by date or member name. <F15> is a toggle key, meaning the display will be sorted by date or by name.

WORKING WITH USER-DEFINED OPTIONS

The Work with User-Defined Options PDM Menu selection allows manipulation of options that are defined in place of or in addition to the options provided by PDM. IBM provides a default file of user-defined commands to which you can add new options. Additional user-defined option files can be created and used. The default user-defined option file is QUAOOPT in library QGPL with member QUAOOPT. This file contains the user-defined options as they are shipped from IBM.

Each user-defined option executes a command. An interface exists between the user-defined option and the information contained within the list entries. Substitution parameters are used to obtain information from the list entry to execute the command.

The following display (Figure 10-3) is shown when a user-defined option file is chosen:

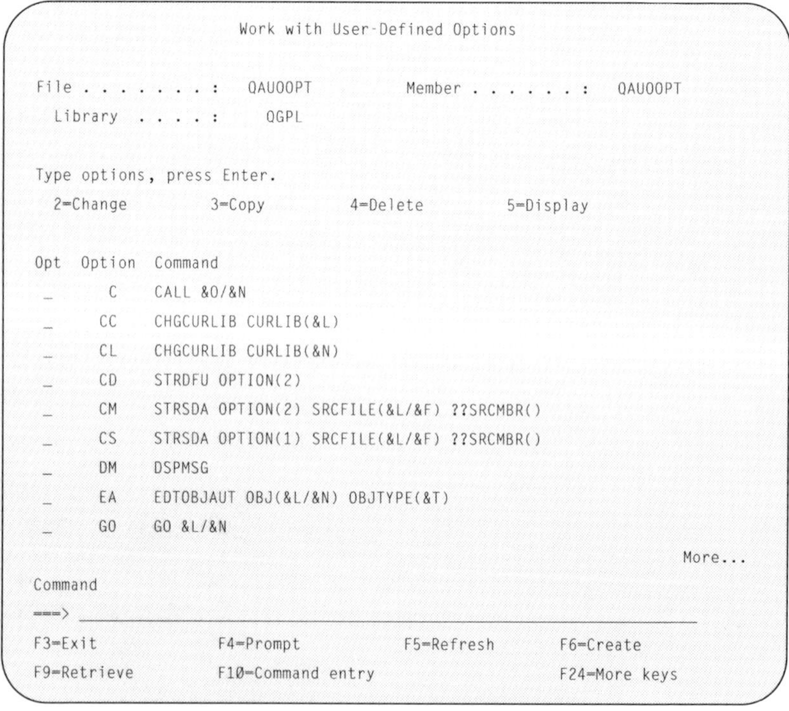

Figure 10-3: Work with User-Defined Options

This display shows the name of the file, library, and member that contains the user-defined options. The display also shows the option and its associated command. Specifying an option in the Opt field allows manipulation of the user-defined options. Option 2 changes an existing user-defined option. Option 3 copies a user-defined option to a different user-defined option. Option 4 deletes a user-defined option. Option 5 displays a user-defined option.

In addition to the options that are available for manipulating user-defined options, the standard, common, and specific function keys are also available. The specific function keys for the Work with User-Defined Options display include <F6>, which creates a new user-defined option, and <F15>, which exits option manipulation without saving changes.

Changing an existing or creating a new user-defined option causes the following screen (Figure 10-4) to be displayed:

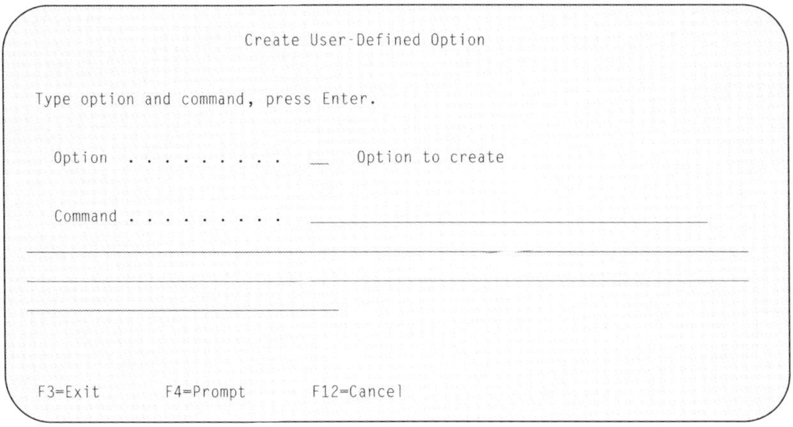

```
                         Create User-Defined Option

  Type option and command, press Enter.

    Option . . . . . . . . .  __   Option to create

    Command . . . . . . . . .  ______________________________



  F3=Exit        F4=Prompt        F12=Cancel
```

Figure 10-4: Create User-Defined Option

The Option parameter can be any character value. Pick a value that describes the action to be taken. The Command parameter can be any command and will be executed when the option is specified next to a list entry.

PDM provides an interface between the list entry and the command through the use of special characters used as substitution parameters. The substitution parameters would then be used as arguments to the command that is to be executed. These special characters are as follows:

&A (Object attribute) — This parameter will be replaced by the object attribute from an entry in a list of objects or have the special value *NULL if not working with a list of objects.

&B (List type) — This substitution parameter will have a value of L if you are working with a list of libraries, O if you are working with a list of objects, M if you are working with a list of members, and X if you are working with a library list.

&C (Option) — This parameter is replaced by the user-defined option code.

&D (Date of last change to the member in the list of members) — The date will be returned in the system date format. This value will be *NULL if you are not working with a list of members.

&E (Run in batch indication) — This substitution parameter will be replaced by *YES if Y is specified on the Change Defaults screen for the Run in batch parameter and *NO if N is specified for the Run in batch parameter.

&F (File name) — This substitution parameter is replaced by the name of the file that contains the members if working with a list of members. This parameter will have a value of *NULL if you are not working with a list of members.

&G (Job description library) — This parameter contains the name of the library associated with the Job description parameter from the Change Defaults screen.

&H (Job description name) — This parameter contains the name of the Job description from the Change Defaults screen.

&J (Job description) — This parameter contains the name of the Job description and the associated Library from the Change Defaults screen in the form of library/jobd.

&L (Library name) — This substitution parameter contains the name of the library that contains the objects or members with which you are working. This parameter will have the value QSYS if you are working with libraries.

&N (Name of the item) — This parameter is replaced by the name of the item in the list.

&O (Object library) — This parameter contains the name of the Object library from the Change Defaults screen.

&P (Compile in batch indication) — This substitution parameter will be replaced by *YES if Y is specified on the Change Defaults screen for the Compile in batch parameter and *NO if N is specified for the Compile in batch parameter.

&R (Replace object indication) — This substitution parameter will be replaced by *YES if Y is specified on the Change Defaults screen for the Replace object parameter and *NO if N is specified for the Replace object parameter.

&S (Item type without *) — This parameter is replaced by LIB if you are working with libraries, by the object type (without the leading *) if you are working with objects or the member type if you are working with members.

&T (Item type with *) — This parameter is replaced by LIB if you are working with libraries, by the object type (with the leading *) if you are working with objects, or the member type if you are working with members.

&U (User-defined option file) — This substitution parameter is replaced by the name of the active user-defined option file. The active user-defined option file is specified on the Change Defaults screen.

&V (User-defined option file library) — This substitution parameter is replaced by the name of the library that contains the active user-defined option file. The active user-defined option file is specified on the Change Defaults screen.

&W (User-defined option file member) — This substitution parameter is replaced by the name of the member that contains the active user-defined options. The active user-defined option file is specified on the Change Defaults screen.

&X (Item text) — This parameter is replaced by the text associated with the list entry. The text is returned to the parameter enclosed in single quotation marks.

CL Programming Operators

The following commands, functions, and operations statements can only be used in formal CL programs (as opposed to being used in command line entry).

CL COMMANDS

CHGVAR ...... Changes the contents of a variable.

CVTDAT .... Converts the format of a date.

DATA .... Indicates the beginning of an inline data file.

DCL .... Declares a variable.

DCLF .... Declares a file to be used.

DMPCLPGM .... Dumps (displays) all variables and all messages on the program message queue to a spooled file.

DO .... Conditionally executes a series of commands.

ELSE .... Provides a conditional course of action. Used with the IF statement.

ENDPGM ...... Ending statement for a CL program.

ENDDO .... Provides the end to a DO group.

ENDRCV....... Ends a request for input. Used with the SNDF, RCVF, and SNDRCVF commands.

GOTO......... Transfers control to a label within the CL program.

IF .... Provides a comparison using CL logical, mathematical, or relational operators.

MONMSG...... Monitors for messages to provide error trapping and recovery functions.

PGM . . . . Beginning statement for a CL program. May optionally include the PARM keyword.

RCVF . . . . Receives information from a database or display file.

RCVMSG. . . . . . . Receives a message from a message queue.

RMVMSG . . . . . . Removes a message from a message queue.

RTVDTAARA . . . Retrieves the contents of the local data area or of a named data area.

RTVJOBA . . . . . . Retrieves the attributes of a job.

RTVMBRD . . . . . Retrieves a member description within a database file.

RTVMSG . . . . Retrieves a message from a message file.

RTVNETA . . . . . . Retrieves the network attributes.

RTVSYSVAL . . . . Retrieves setting for a specified system value.

RTVUSRPRF . . . . Retrieves attributes contained in a user profile.

SNDF . . . . Sends information to a display file.

SNDRCVF . . . . . . Sends then retrieves information to and from a display file.

SNDPGMMSG. . . Sends a message to a message queue.

SNDUSRMSG . . . Sends a message to a user message queue.

SNDRPY . . . . Sends a reply to an inquiry message.

TRFCTL . . . . Transfer control to a program.

WAIT . . . . Waits for a information to be received from a database file or a display file. Used with the SNDF, RCVF, or SNDRCVF commands.

CL FUNCTIONS

%SUBSTRING . . . Extracts a substring from a character variable. May be abbreviated as %SST. The syntax is %SUBSTRING(<string> <start> <length>).

%SWITCH . . . . . Compares the settings of execution switches with a mask composed of a series of 8 bytes with possible values of 1 (on), 0 (off), or X (don't care). The syntax is %SWITCH(<mask>).

CL LOGICAL OPERATORS

*AND . . . . Logical AND

*OR . . . . Logical OR

*NOT . . . . Logical NOT

CL RELATIONAL OPERATORS

> or *GT . . . . . . Greater Than

< or *LT . . . . Less Than

= or *EQ . . . . . . Equal To

>= or *GE . . . . . . Greater Than or Equal To

<= or *LE . . . . . . Less Than or Equal To

<> or *NE . . . . . . Not Equal To

CL MATHEMATICAL OPERATORS

+ . . . . Addition

- . . . . Subtraction

* . . . . Multiplication

/ . . . . Division

CL STRING OPERATORS

*CAT . . . . Concatenates two string variables together with no intervening spaces.

*BCAT . . . . Concatenates two string variables together with one blank space in between.

*TCAT . . . . Concatenates two string variables together and trims trailing spaces from the first variable.

CL SPECIAL PURPOSE PROGRAMS

QCMDEXC . . . . . Executes a single command from within a CL program.

QCMDCHK . . . . Checks the syntax of a single command and optionally prompts the command.

QCLSCAN . . . . . Scans a string of characters to determine if a specified substring exists.

QDCXLATE . . . . Translates between different character codes.

Types of Objects

All objects on the AS/400 or organized into pre-defined types. Information on object type assignments can be obtained through the WRKOBJ command.

*ALRTBL . . . . . . Alert table

*AUTL . . . . Authorization list

*CLD . . . . C locale description

*CHTFMT . . . . . Chart format

*CLS . . . . Class

*COSD . . . . Class-of-service description

*CMD . . . . Command

*CNNL . . . . Connection list

*CFGL . . . . Configuration list

*CTLD . . . . Controller description

*CSPMAP . . . . . . Cross-system product map

*CSI . . . . Communications side information

*CSPTBL . . . . Cross-system product table

*DTAARA . . . . . . Data area

*DTADCT . . . . . . Data dictionary

*DTAQ . . . . Data queue

*DEVD . . . . Device description

*DOC . . . . Document

*EDTD . . . . Edit description

*FNTRSC . . . . . . Font resource

*FCT. . . . . Forms control table

*FILE . . . . File

*FLR. . . . . Folder

*FORMDF . . . . . Form definition

*GSS . . . . Graphics symbol set

*IGCSRT. . . . . . . Double-byte character set sort table

*IGCTBL. . . . . . . Double-byte character set font table

*IGCDCT . . . . . . Double-byte conversion dictionary

*JOBD. . . . . Job description

*JOBQ . . . . Job queue

*JRN . . . . Journal

*JRNRCV . . . . . . Journal receiver

*LIB . . . . Library

*LIND. . . . . Line description

*MENU. . . . . Menu

*MODD . . . . Mode description

*MSGF . . . . Message file

*MSGQ. . . . . Message queue

*NWID . . . . Network identifier

*OUTQ. . . . . Output queue

*OVL . . . . Overlay

*PAGDFN . . . . . . Page definition

*PAGSEG . . . . . . Page segment

*PDG . . . . Print descriptor group

*PNLGRP . . . . . . Panel group

*PRDAVL . . . . . . Product availability

*PRDDFN . . . . . . Product definition

*PRDLOD . . . . . . Product load

*PGM . . . . Program

*QRYDFN . . . . . . Query definition

*QMFORM . . . . . Query management form

*QMQRY . . . . . . Query management query

*RCT . . . . Reference code translate table

*S36 . . . . System/36 machine description

*SBSD . . . . Subsystem description

*SCHIDX . . . . . . Information search index

*SPADCT . . . . . . Spelling aid dictionary

*SQLPKG . . . . . . Structured query language package

*SSND . . . . Session description

*TBL . . . . Table

*USRIDX . . . . . . User index

*USRPRF . . . . . . User profile

*USRQ . . . . User queue

*USRSPC . . . . . . User space

Note that objects types *AUTL, *COSD, *CTLD, *DEVD, *LIB, *LIND, *MODD, and *USRPRF reside in the QSYS library. Objects types *DOC and *FLR reside in the QDOC library. All other objects can be assigned to libraries when created.

APPENDIX C

Object and File Attributes

In addition to being classified by type, objects may be further divided into groups based on attribute assignments. Also note that many of these same attributes are directly applicable to files. The following list shows the attributes that can be associated with objects. Those attributes that are also applicable to files (object type *FILE) are marked with an asterisk after the attribute name:

BAS . . . . BASIC program

BAS36 . . . . System/36 BASIC program

BAS38 . . . . System/38 BASIC program

BSCF38* . . . . System/38 bisync communications file

C. . . . . C program

CBL. . . . . COBOL program

CBL36 . . . . System/36 COBOL program

CBL38. . . . . System/38 COBOL program

CLP . . . . Control Language program

CLP38 . . . . System/38 Control Language program

CMD . . . . Command

CMD38 . . . . System/38 command

CMNF38* . . . . . . System/38 communications file

CSPAE . . . . Cross-System Product application execution

DDMF* . . . . Distributed Data Management file

DFU* . . . . Data File Utility file

DFUEXEC* . . . . . Data File Utility executable file

DFUNOTEXC* . . Data File Utility non-executable file

DKTF* . . . . Diskette file

DSPF* . . . . Display file

DSPF36 . . . . System/36 display file

DSPF38* . . . . System/38 display file

FTN . . . . FORTRAN program

ICFF* . . . . Inter-System Communications Function file

LF* . . . . Logical file

LF38* . . . . System/38 logical file

MXDF38* . . . . . . System/38 mixed file

PAS . . . . Pascal program

PF* . . . . Physical file (source or data)

PF38* . . . . System/38 physical file

PLI . . . . PL/1 program

PLI38 . . . . System/38 PL/1 program

PRTF* . . . . Printer file

PRTF38* . . . . System/38 printer file

QRY38 . . . . System/38 Query

RMC . . . . RM/COBOL program

RPG . . . . RPG program

RPG36 . . . . System/36 RPG program

RPG38 . . . . System/38 RPG program

RPT . . . . RPG auto report

RPT36 . . . . System/36 RPG auto report

RPT38 . . . . System/38 RPG auto report

SAVF* . . . . Save file

SPADCT . . . . Spelling aid dictionary

SQLC . . . . Structured Query Language C program

SQLCBL . . . . Structured Query Language COBOL program

SQLFTN . . . . Structured Query Language FORTRAN program

SQLPLI . . . . Structured Query Language PL/1 program

SQLRPG . . . . Structured Query Language RPG program

TAPF* . . . . Tape file

TBL . . . . Table

Types of Members

Like objects, members can be broken down into different types. Note that they are similar but not identical to the object attributes. The following member types are supported:

BAS . . . . BASIC program

BAS36 . . . . System/36 BASIC program

BAS38 . . . . System/38 BASIC program

BASP . . . . BASIC procedure

BASP38 . . . . System/38 BASIC procedure

C. . . . . C program

CBL. . . . . COBOL program

CBL36. . . . . System/36 COBOL program

CBL38. . . . . System/38 COBOL program

CLD . . . . C locale description

CLP . . . . Control Language program

CLP38. . . . . System/38 Control Language program

CMD . . . . OS/400 command

CMD38 . . . . System/38 command

DSPF. . . . . Display file

DSPF36. . . . . System/36 display file

DSPF38. . . . . System/38 display file

FTN . . . . FORTRAN program

ICFF . . . . Inter-System Communications Function file

LF . . . . Logical file

LF38 . . . . System/38 logical file

MNU . . . . Menu

MNUCMD . . . . . Menu command file

MNUDDS . . . . . . Menu DDS

MNU36 . . . . System/36 menu

MSGF36 . . . . System/36 message file

OCL36 . . . . System/36 Operator Control Language

PAS . . . . Pascal program

PF . . . . Physical file (source or data)

PF38 . . . . System/38 physical file

PLI . . . . PL/1 program

PLI38 . . . . System/38 PL/1 program

PNLGRP . . . . Panel group

PRTF . . . . Printer file

PRTF38 . . . . System/38 printer file

QRY38 . . . . System/38 Query

REXX . . . . Restructured Extended Executor Language procedure

RMC . . . . RM/COBOL program

RPG . . . . RPG program

RPG36 . . . . System/36 RPG program

RPG38 . . . . System/38 RPG program

RPT . . . . RPG Auto Report program

RPT36 . . . . System/36 RPG Auto Report program

RPT38 . . . . System/38 RPG Auto Report program

SPADCT . . . . Spelling aid dictionary

SQLC . . . . Structured Query Language C program

SQLCBL . . . . Structured Query Language COBOL program

SQLFTN . . . . Structured Query Language FORTRAN program

SQLPLI . . . . Structured Query Language PL/1 program

SQLRPG . . . . Structured Query Language RPG program

TBL . . . . Table

TXT . . . . Text

Common Workstation Error Codes

0000 . . . . <HELP> key pressed, but no help is available.

0001 . . . . The AS/400 lost the last character you entered.

0002 . . . . You input an invalid character code.

0003 . . . . <ALT> key used with an invalid key.

0004 . . . . You attempted to input data in a protected area.

0007 . . . . Failure to input data in a mandatory- enter field (**).

0010 . . . . You tried to input alphabetic data in a numeric field.

0011 . . . . Attempt to input data in the sign area of a numeric field.

0012 . . . . You tried to insert data at the end of a field.

0013 . . . . You tried to exit a field after pressing <INSERT>.

0014 . . . . You attempted to exit a mandatory- fill(*) field.

0015 . . . . Failure to enter a self-check field correctly.

0016 . . . . You pressed <FIELD->, but the field is not numeric.

0017 . . . . Attempt to Field Exit out of a mandatory-fill (*) field.

0018 . . . . You pressed an illegal key to exit the field.

0019 . . . . You pressed <DUP> key in a field that doesn't support it.

0020 . . . . You pressed an illegal key for the field.

0021 . . . . You attempted to skip a mandatory-enter field (**).

0022 .... Miscellaneous system error.

0023 .... Illegal use of the Hex function.

0026 .... You pressed <FIELD->, but the last character is not numeric.

0027 .... You pressed an unsupported key.

0028 .... You pressed an unsupported key.

0029 .... Illegal key in a multikey sequence.

0040-0054 ..... Data communications failure.

0099 .... Attempt to use a function that requires you to be signed on.

9001-9010 ..... Invalid operation during Record or Play function.

9012 .... Invalid key used during Setup function.

9015 .... Illegal use of the Quit function.

9016 .... You pressed an illegal combination of several keys.

9019 .... Invalid key used during Record or Play function.

9030 .... Jump function not available for your workstation.

9051 .... Illegal key pressing during Printer Setup function.

9052 .... Printer not ready (or out of paper).

(*)........... A mandatory-fill field must be completely filled or left entirely blank.

(**).......... A mandatory-enter field must receive data input (but it does not have to be completely filled).

Index

D

E

F

G

H

S

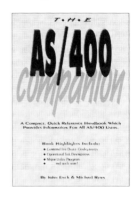

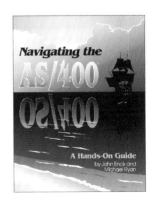

CBM Books Order Form

To order by mail, complete and return the form below.

Title	Qty	Subtotal
The AS/400 Companion		
1-5 books **$19.00 each**		
6-15 books **$16.15 each**		
16-49 books **$13.30 each**		
50+ books **$11.40 each**		
Navigating the AS/400: A Hands On Guide		
1-5 books **$39.00 each**		
6-15 books **$33.15 each**		
16-49 books **$27.30 each**		
50+ books **$23.40 each**		
PA residents add 6% sales tax.		
Handling Charge		$1.50
UPS shipping: $4 for the first book, $1 for each additional book. Outside the U.S., please call (215) 643-8105 for shipping information.		
TOTAL ORDER		

Save up to 40%

Name ______________________________

Title ______________________________

Company ______________________________

Address ______________________________
(Street address required.)

City ______________________________ State ________ Zip ____________

Country ______________________________

Telephone (______) ____________________ FAX (______) ____________________

Payment enclosed $________________. (payable to Cardinal Business Media, Inc.)

Charge to: ☐ MasterCard ☐ VISA ☐ American Express

Account # ______________________________ Exp. Date ____________

Signature ______________________________ Date ____________

ASCB1094

☐ **Please send me a FREE CBM Books Catalog.**

Mail to: CBM Books
1300 Virginia Drive, Suite 400
Fort Washington, PA 19034